A Man's Guide to Newborn Babies

How to Thrive As A New Father When Baby Arrives!

Anthony Kim

Toronto, Canada

Disclaimer

The information provided in this book is designed to provide helpful information on the transition into fatherhood, and related subjects. This book is not meant to be used, nor should it be used, to diagnose or treat any medical condition of the reader or family members. For diagnosis or treatment of a medical condition or problem, please consult your own physician. The publisher and author are not responsible for any specific allergy or other health needs that may require medical attention or supervision and are not liable for any damages or negative consequences from any action, lack of action, application, treatment, or preparation to any person reading or following the information in this book. References are provided for informational purposes only and do not constitute endorsement of any websites, products, books, or other sources.

This book is sold with the understanding that the author or publisher is not engaged to render any type of medical, psychological, legal, or any other kind of professional advice.

ISBN-10: 1521163065

ISBN-13: 978-1521163061

Author's website: www.ADadsGuide.org

For my beautiful daughter Victoria.

About me

Hi! I'm Anthony Kim and thank you for purchasing my book!

I live in Toronto, Canada with my lovely wife Yuri and beautiful baby girl Victoria. I have a busy and fulfilling career as a medical physicist specializing in radiation oncology. I am also an assistant professor at the University of Toronto.

Although I am always busy with parenting and work I keep extra busy with crazy projects like writing this how-to baby book for guys. I have written my first sci-fi novel, something that I have always wanted to do (check it out at www.comaimprisonment.com). I also have started my parenting blog at ADadsGuide.org. I like lifting weights, reading books, and playing with my cute baby girl whenever I can.

Also by Anthony Kim

Non-Fiction

A Dad's Guide to Great Sleep

A Dad's Guide to Saving Money When Baby Arrives
*(**FREE eBook** at ADadsGuide.org/free-ebooks)*

Fiction

Coma Imprisonment

Coma Imprisonment: Revolutions
(FREE web serial novel at ComaImprisonment.com)

Table of Contents

Introduction

On Mother's Day, my baby girl Victoria came into the world and I was a new father. It was the happiest day of my life. I held this blue-gray, shriveled, hairy, cross-eyed little human being in my arms and thought that she was the most beautiful thing in the world.

Then, a whirlwind of events whipped by: doctors stitched up my wife, nurses measured our baby, orderlies cleaned up what looked like a murder scene, and relatives visited my new family. We were whisked off to the maternity section. A trio of no-nonsense nurses with thick eastern European accents very rapidly did their checks and left us to our own devices.

Everything quickly devolved into confusion as to what the heck I should do now. All of the books, websites, and advice from family and friends pretty much went out the window and my wife and I had to figure a lot of things out for ourselves.

From then until the completion of the first draft of this book, it has been four months since Victoria was born and I feel like I learned a colossal amount about how to be a dad to a newborn baby.

There is so much stuff out there to prepare a couple for when a baby arrives. I consumed this stuff. "What To Expect When You're Expecting", "The Happiest Baby on the Block", WebMD's excellent website on babies and pregnancy—all these resources contain really great stuff you definitely need to know.

Even with all of this knowledge available, there was a pretty glaring omission in the literature. What became pretty clear to me before and after our baby was born was how little material there was out there geared towards how new dads can be the best that they can be during the transition into fatherhood.

Luckily for us, my wife and I hit the learning curve hard and figured things out rapidly. We quickly adjusted to our new reality and became a happy and functional family.

I am not sure that this is the experience of a lot of new dads. A lot of the fathers that I talked to before Victoria's birth actually had quite a lot of negative things to say about taking care of babies—sleep deprivation, cranky wives, loss of freedom, you name it. I often hear new dads and moms swear off having another child because of all the difficulties they had with their first. I think that it is a tragedy that some first-time parents decide not to have more children just because they could not figure out how to take care of babies effectively, efficiently, and with minimal stress.

There are lots of unwanted consequences from not knowing how to make the transition to parenthood smoothly. Marital strife, financial difficulties, stress, depression, and sleeplessness are the fallout from an inability to deal with the additional responsibilities of having a child. I strongly believe that a baby's development is negatively impacted by stressed-out, over-worked, and overwhelmed parents. It is an unfortunate reality that many children are held back in their personal growth because their parents lack information on how to do the job efficiently.

But it really doesn't have to be this way. As a new dad, you have the power to guide your new family smoothly through the transition period after your baby is born. There are dozens of life hacks that a new dad can do before and after the birth that can make taking care of a newborn a thousand times easier. I think it is really important to try to minimize the challenges so that you can fully enjoy the rather wonderful experience of being a father to a newborn baby. I want to tell the next new father I meet that having a baby is a transcendently happy experience, not a miserable slog. I want to tell that guy who is scared of having a kid that once optimized systems are in place, everything will be just fine.

The reason why I sat down to write this book is because everyone was saying how unusually well-rested and happy I was when my baby was born. Some people were actually annoyed at my buoyant behaviour, especially the ones who warned me before Victoria's birth about how miserable and sleep-deprived I would be. My wife was handling things well with the sudden changes in her life. My baby was thriving—all indicators such as weight gain, head size, and height were following normal trajectories and she was ahead of the curve when it came to developmental milestones. I figured that I was doing something right and wanted to share it with as many guys as possible.

One of the things that I really found important is to take care of ALL three people in your family—your baby, your wife, and you. I strongly suggest that you take the lead in taking care of the physical and mental health of your wife, who just got her ass kicked by passing a whole human being through her "down there". It is also very important to take care of you. As a new dad, you have to be the rock in the family. Wife-care and self-care are synergistic with your baby's well-being.

This book is essentially a collection of life hacks for new dads that is divided into three parts: **self-care**, **wife-care**, and **baby-care**.

Self-care is vital as you have to be the rock of the family for the first few months while your baby is totally helpless and your wife is recovering physically and emotionally from the insane trauma of giving birth.

Wife-care must be guided by you as your wife will instinctively want to take care of the baby ahead of taking care of herself—you need to wrestle down the maternal instinct a little bit in order to make sure your wife is happy and healthy.

The last part of this book is on **baby-care**. This part has a slew of life hacks to make the care and feeding of a newborn as efficient as possible.

Things change pretty quickly with the baby's development. The content in this book focuses on the first three months after birth but is still largely applicable up to age six months. I do not offer any specific medical advice for your baby or your wife beyond the obvious stuff (breast milk is best, make sure you exercise, and such); rather, this book is meant as a guide to make your transition into parenthood as smooth and enjoyable as possible.

Make the transition to fatherhood thrive-able, not just survivable. I really hope this helps you guys in this excellent new phase of life!

Part 1

Self-care:

Be the rock!

Adopt a positive mental attitude

Before the baby comes, it is a great idea to get your mental self in top gear. The mental game is important to get right because with a positive mental attitude the work feels a lot lighter.

The first thing to do is to clear your head of the negative things that people will tell you about having a baby. These kinds of thoughts will not help you. For me, it was a little disheartening to hear all of the negative commentary from parents about how hard it was to raise a baby. When we were telling everyone about my wife's pregnancy, among the congratulations came the dire warnings from guys:

- "After the baby is born, sleep will be a far distant memory."
- "Having a baby is the hardest thing you will ever do!"
- "Oh, the diapers, so many diapers…" (devolving to unmanly sobbing into hands).

This sort of talk dominated as we approached our due date. It was like some men couldn't say anything positive about having a newborn baby. I understand that everyone was just trying to get us prepared for what would undoubtedly be a lot of hard work and responsibility, but it was a downer to be hearing this stuff all the time. Everyone was so focused on how bad the sleep deprivation was!

Then there were the few guys who really stood out in the things that they would say:

- "Being a father is a wonderful experience, I hope you and your wife enjoy this time in your life."
- "That's such exciting news! You should take advantage of the nice weather and go for some nice light walks with the baby and wife so that it gets her blood flowing."
- "Becoming a father was the best thing to ever happen to me."

I preferred to focus on these encouraging words instead of the doom and gloom! So leading up to the pregnancy I decided to drop from my mind all of the warnings about sleep deprivation and the hardship of diaper changing and simply adopt a positive mental attitude about the whole journey.

At that point I realized that I had a choice how to adopt my mindset: either I would choose to believe that baby-care is a thankless, God-forsaken task, or I would hold in my mind that everything that I do to raise my child would be the best calling that I can possibly answer in this world.

I am sure that the latter approach is the best way to become an awesome father and husband.

So, up until the birth I would just make light of anyone who tried to warn me about the sleepless nights, endless diaper changes, and loss of freedom. I would say stuff like "What, you expect me to back out of this thing now? The train has left the station!" I would also say in a deep, manly voice "I fear nothing—even small, needy babies."

I am sure that everyone who was warning us about all the work that a baby entails has the best intentions, but negative comments were really not helpful. I think that the most helpful thing to say to a new parent is:

"All the hard work is a joy to do in order to have the most excellent and rewarding experience of your life—being a parent."

Feel a deep sense of gratitude

It is an incredible coincidence that your baby even exists. Think of all of the things that led to this pivotal moment in human history, the birth of your baby.

1. You and your wife had to meet, fall in love, and do something to create a baby.
2. You and your wife had to separately evade disease and disaster to make it to reproductive age.
3. You and your wife's parents each had to meet, fall in love, do something to make a baby, and evade disease and disaster to get to reproductive age.
4. Every generation before you had to make it to adulthood and raise weakling babies in the presence of really insane stuff like bubonic plague, medieval warfare, drought, famine, and sabre-toothed tigers.
5. Man had to evolve from primitive apes.
6. Apes had to evolve from even more primitive lifeforms.
7. Deoxyribonucleic acid somehow had to order itself from the primordial ooze.
8. Earth had to develop the correct chemistry to develop primordial ooze.

9. The solar system had to create the symphony of planets and moons at exactly the right orbits for Earth to become a candidate for life.
10. Stars had to form complex elements inside their core to support life's eventual complexity.
11. The Big Bang had to be just hot enough and expand just fast enough to create stars with the potential to form complex elements.
12. Probably even more improbable stuff had to happen before the Big Bang for that event to occur.

The fact that your baby exists is a colossal mind-blowingly amazing miracle. Everything had to go right for a very long time for your baby to happen.

At a less cosmic scale, it is a very lucky thing to be able to have a child. Many people in this world are infertile due to congenital defects, lifestyle choices, disease burden, and other unfortunate circumstances. Many people find it very difficult to find a partner with whom they can form a bond strong enough to pursue parenthood. I know that I had my own challenges in meeting someone who I wanted to marry and have children with, so I ended up looking for the right girl for a long time.

I am thankful every day for being able to have a child. I keep an electronic journal in Word where I write down three things that I am grateful for at the start of every day. Having a family is always on that list.

Gratitude is like a titanium shield—it protects you from all of that life throws at you. It can even convert bad stuff into something positive, kind of like bad-stuff alchemy. If you are grateful every day and every moment of your child's life, you will consider it a privilege and an honor to clean up her poop and settle her screaming.

Gratitude works for a lot of things in life. Having it makes for a happier man.

Have a lot of faith in yourself

"Whether you think you can, or you think you can't—you're right." -Henry Ford

If you believe that you can do a thing, then you can probably do that thing. So, if you think you can raise a child, then you can do it. Fortunately, your baby has basically already made the choice for you—the baby is on its way and you have no option but to be the best damn dad you can be.

It is exceedingly possible to raise a healthy child. Some perspective on this: at the time of this writing, 108 billion people have been born on this planet.

108 billion babies!

Lots of those people got to the point of giving birth to a child of their own. The parents of these 108 billion babies include people who were trying to raise kids 20,000 years ago while being chased by megafauna, while being forced to build giant pyramids for some egomaniacal Pharoah, during the depths of the Dark Ages, during the time of the Black Plague in Europe, and while enduring the mortal danger of a modern war zone. My point is that all these people found a way to raise their kids with a pretty high success rate so this thing is eminently doable.

Another thing that might give perspective is that all of the things that you were warned about—sleep deprivation, endless crying, and diaper changing—is probably not as difficult as many other challenges that you have had in your life. By now, you have become a man of worth. Think of the difficulties you went through in building your career, finding a home, and courting your wife. Having a baby is just another challenge that you need to figure out.

I can tell you that I was *way* more sleep-deprived during my university days in mechanical engineering than I am right now taking care of a newborn. The crying is not so bad once I honed my weapons-of-choice to calm a fussy baby (more on that in the chapter on calming techniques later on). You will be very surprised at how little time diapers really take—we'll review that later as well.

Think of any challenges that you overcame in your past, like getting over a broken relationship, the death of a loved one, losing a job, or getting through school. You might find that taking care of a baby is a very doable enterprise compared to your former life challenges.

Gentlemen, having a baby is not that hard. If you are concerned about your ability to care for a child, know that the cures to fear are education and action. Reading this book is the education; implementing the life hacks in this book is the action.

Figure out the price to pay and pay it

This is how I live my life now: I figure out what I want, figure out the price of that thing, and if I still want it I pay the price. The formula to get what you want in life goes like this:

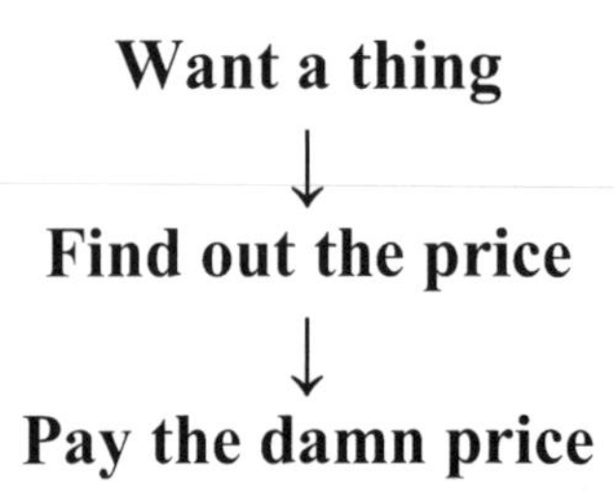

Having a child in your life follows the same simple formula. Figure out if you want a kid. The price is the commitment it takes to raising a kid, which is considerable; however, you could look at it as a rewarding task if you set your mind to that approach.

The reward is immeasurable: you have someone to carry out your legacy, you have the unmatched experience of becoming a parent, you have someone who will love you no matter what (well, this is true as long as you don't totally screw it up), and you will have someone to hold your hand as they push you through the doors to surgery. The return on investment is "infinity" divided by "a lot of work". So, ROI is basically infinity.

It is also good to realize that a lot of the freedoms you enjoyed without a child in your life will be significantly curtailed. For at least the first six months, you cannot go out to the pub, you have to maximize the time you spend at home, and you have to give up a lot of your leisure activities. This is part of the price, but you knew that when you decided to have a kid. You did consciously decide to have a baby, right??

When I became a parent, I realized that all of the freedoms and comfort I enjoyed in my pre-baby life were replaced with better things: the joys of raising a child, personal growth elicited by the increased responsibility, paradoxically more free time since I was forced to optimize my schedule, and the drive to work on projects that were important to me such as this book. Having a baby was ultimately important in my growth as a person and allowed me to take my life to the next level. Giving up your life from before to sculpt a new life with your growing family is not really giving up anything at all. It is actually the next step in your personal evolution.

Once you made the choice to have a baby, figure out if you want to pay the price, then pay it. Pretty simple formula, right?

Tune the machine: Keep your body healthy

Running parallel to getting your mind right, you need to get physically fit as well before the baby is born. Working on your physical fitness is one of the best investments you could possibly make for your life to go smoothly after the baby arrives.

The main reason why you need to have your body functioning well is because you will be moving, lifting, squatting, and running around a lot more than in your pre-baby life. During the first six weeks of baby's life you will be doing nearly all of the heavy lifting required to run the house and take care of the baby as your wife recovers from birth. Beyond six weeks, even though the chores will slowly get rebalanced between you and your wife, your baby will gain weight and will require some solid strength and fitness to deal with the extra physical workload.

After birth, your wife will have gone through a hell of a physical trial. There are hormones that cause the pelvic bone ligaments to relax in order to stretch enough for the baby to pass through—these hormones also create systemic joint pain that makes it difficult for a new mother to do any heavy lifting. Your wife's "down there" will also have gone through trauma including possible skin and muscle tearing, with the attendant stitches. Basically, your wife can handle the breastfeeding but not much else for the first little while. You need to be in shape to meet the challenge of taking up the slack.

If you normally work out, this is perfect. If you are a bit out of shape, then you will need some time to get fit prior to the main event. It takes at least a couple of months to go from couch potato to what I call "reasonably fit". To me, this means you can do nominal exercise challenges like doing 20 push ups in a row, running three miles without barfing, and getting down to a healthy weight.

This is not hard to do. Moderate exercise such as running, walking, weight-lifting, home-video workouts, and taking care of yard work are all really great to get you up to speed. Start walking to where you need to go instead of driving. Take a stroll outside in the middle of your work day. I did some online video workouts, went out for light jogs, and dropped down and did twenty push-ups every now and then. Getting ready for baby care is not quite at the same level as training for a marathon, but you do really need to get nominally fit in order to take on life after the baby arrives.

One thing that will help you get fit before baby and also help with calming her down is a stability ball—more on that in the chapter on infant calming techniques later on. Get a stability ball if you do not have one. They are fantastic for core exercises, calming the baby, and for older kids to play with.

It is a very good idea to get fit *before* baby arrives onto the scene. After the baby arrives you will have less time to dedicate to working out solo.

Optimize, Optimize, Optimize

Optimize your time. Optimize your work. Optimize your household. It is best to do this prior to the baby's birth.

Sit down with a notepad and pen. Think of all the ways that you can save time and energy. Think of the ways that you can increase productivity. Write them down neatly and concisely so that you can refer to these tactics to keep yourself on track.

Here are some methods that you might consider during this exercise:

Batch process everything

I work in health care, where I have clinical days and project days. After my kid was born, I batched all of the clinical days together so that I would have long, uninterrupted weeks working on projects so that I can maintain my persistence of concentration. This vastly improved my efficiency at work, resulting in fewer work hours.

At home, I batched all of my chores (dishes, vacuuming, taking out the garbage, etc) for after dinner so that everything got done all at once and faster than if the tasks were split up.

You can batch process lots of things: do all the yard work at once, buy bulk groceries at Costco so you don't have to go shopping as often, have a bunch of visitors come and see baby instead of one at a time, and cook in huge batches and freeze the leftovers for easy re-heating.

Stop watching TV

This alone will give you the extra time you need for baby care. The average Canadian spends 30 hours a week watching television, according to a recent study by the Bureau of Broadcast Measurement Canada. I am pretty sure most developed nations have similar statistics.

Thirty hours of TV is a pretty hefty chunk of time. You could even work a second job or start a home-based business with that amount of time. Re-dedicate TV time to baby care, other projects around the house, or generating another income. Imagine all the stuff you can get done.

Get to work and leave work 30 minutes earlier

This tactic will have you beat rush hour both ways. This tactic saved me around 20 minutes per day, or 100 minutes a week.

"Early to bed, early to rise makes a man healthy, wealthy, and wise."

This excellent quote from Benjamin Franklin holds especially true for new dads. After my Victoria was born, I started waking up at 5-6 A.M. in order to do things like write this book and lift weights at the gym. Waking up early allows you to get a lot done while mom and baby are still asleep.

Morning is when your mental acuity is at its best so use it wisely. Do the work that requires the most brainpower right after rising.

Find ways to utilize every spare minute of the day

It is amazing how much you can squeeze into the day in between feedings and diaper changes. I used small slivers of time to peck away at this book as well as complete a slew of home improvement projects and also working on a home-based business with my wife.

Eliminate social media

What? Get rid of Facebook when you're having a baby?? I know that you probably think I am nuts. Well, there are many well-documented reasons to get off of social media.

For one, it makes you feel worse to look at it, because it is hard to compare your everyday life to everyone else's highlight reel.

But the main reason to ditch social media when you are about to have a baby is because it is a massive time suck. Pour that time into reading to your newborn or hitting on your wife to make her feel more attractive. If you absolutely need to jump on your social media platforms from time to time, schedule time for it at the end of the day as evenings are when your brain is least capable of cognitively demanding activities.

This exercise of writing down and enacting how to optimize your world can be repeated again and again after the baby is born so that you are constantly fine-tuning your new life.

Detox and energize

When the baby is born, you will need to have high, stable energy levels.

It is no good to rely upon caffeine, sugar, or adrenaline spikes when you are trying to care for a baby, hold down your day job/business, and run the household.

The best way to manage your energy levels is to detoxify your mind and body, and to find sustainable energy sources to run your physical systems. The way to do this is to adopt good habits and get rid of bad habits to support your efforts.

There are a number of things you can do to detox and energize your mind and body so that both will run at optimal levels.

Quit coffee

Quit coffee? You're probably calling me extra-crazy right now. I just told you to quit TV and social media, and now I'm telling you to give up coffee?

Quitting coffee actually is one of great things that you can do to increase your energy throughout the day. This is counter-intuitive but true. When you drink coffee, a huge spike of caffeine hits your brain like a runaway train. You are hyper-alert for perhaps an hour, but without an additional hit of caffeine you will quickly crash.

Too much coffee interferes with your sleep as well. If you do not sleep well, you are less likely to exercise. The drop in energy from lack of exercise will make you crave more coffee, and on and on in a vicious circle.

Quitting coffee decreases anxiety, reduces stress, and lowers blood pressure. It improves your mood and mellows you out.

I was a coffee drinker for many, many years. I loved the stuff. I was getting to the point where I was drinking two to three mega cups of coffee a day. One day I just decided to give up coffee because I wanted to sleep better and thought that it would help with my mental focus. After powering through four days of caffeine-withdrawal headaches, I was sleeping much better and had laser-like focus. My wife noticed the change in me and said that I became a better husband. As of this writing I have been off coffee for eight months and definitely have no intention of going back.

Switch to green tea, which has one third of the caffeine in it. The antioxidants in green tea also do a body good. The caffeine high from tea is much milder and longer lasting than from coffee. I switched to tea and am happier for it. The mild caffeine buzz from tea is just enough to kickstart my day.

If you quit coffee, do it before the baby. Remember my experience: you have to pound through four days of caffeine withdrawal headaches once you quit. Believe me though, quitting coffee is worth it and will do wonders for your energy levels, which helps enormously when caring for a baby.

Cut down on beer

Alcohol is a depressant. It robs you of energy. That is why guys drink it, to wind down after a hectic day. With a baby in the mix, beer works against you. I did not quit beer altogether, but I did cut down quite a lot. Like quitting coffee, quitting or cutting down on beer will help with your energy levels, you will sleep better, and your mood will improve.

Other side effects of culling beer from your diet include: weight loss, better skin, less midnight snacking, more money in your wallet, and more intense workouts.

Go for walks

Get out there. Breathe outdoor air and get some exercise. Be alone with your thoughts. This calms the mind and focuses energy.

The greatest minds in history have all expressed how walking re-energizes their minds and bodies. Charles Darwin took three walks a day along a path through Sandwalk Wood near his home in England while working out his theory on the transmutation of species. Ludwig van Beethoven regularly took quick jaunts outside to take a break from his composition work to enliven his spirit. Steve Jobs often went for long walks to stoke his creativity and ended up taking over the world with technology.

Walking is rejuvenating to anyone who faces an important task. I often pace around in my backyard when I need a break from taking care of my baby. I often take my baby with me for a stroll around the block to give both of us a break from being indoors. Going for walks outdoors does wonders for energizing your mind, body, and spirit.

Take cold showers

Hot showers are actually a pretty recent innovation. Throughout human history, people have taken cold showers for health and rejuvenation.

Cold showers are refreshing. Cold showers improve cardiovascular health, skin tone, and mental acuity. Cold showers have even shown to improve your immune system and stimulate weight loss. Any athlete can attest to how cold showers can help you recover faster from muscle soreness and fatigue. I take a cold shower every day before I go to work. It supercharges my body and readies my mind for the rigors of the day ahead.

You will be sold on cold showers once you get used to them. If going cold all the way is too much, try a contrast shower: start cold, heat up the water, and end cold.

Eat healthy food and drink water

Your body works well if good food and drink goes into it. The converse is also true: if you put junk in, then you will feel like junk.

Energize your body by feeding it excellent, healthy food. I am not a dietician but I know what healthy food is. Almost everyone knows what healthy food is because the basics are incredibly simple. Eat your fruits and vegetables. Eat clean protein like steak, eggs, pork, and chicken. Drink water. Avoid processed foods and sugar. If you eat and drink like this, you are most of the way to a great diet. The rest is fine tuning (i.e. how many times a day do you eat, how much you eat per meal, that sort of thing).

You have to trick yourself into eating healthy food. To do that you need to build a system. The system at my house is simple: have lots of healthy food either prepped up or easy to cook in the fridge. My wife and I have a mostly Korean diet. Korean food is great for two reasons: it is quite healthy and you can store bulk Korean dishes in the fridge for quite a long time because much of it is naturally preserved with onion, garlic, chili pepper, brine, and soy sauce. A typical dinner prep consists of taking out a bunch of preserved side dishes, frying up some beef, pork, tofu, or chicken, and making a simple soup with fish broth and Asian vegetables. Total prep time is typically twenty minutes because the elements of our dinner are already prepared or are very easy to put together.

Keep lots of water in the fridge so that you can enjoy cold water whenever you want. By having a ready supply of cold, delicious water on hand, you will be less likely to drink soda or juice. Speaking of which, evict soda and juice from your refrigerator. I keep bottles of water around to take with me to the gym or when the family and I are out to avoid the temptation of buying over-priced sugary drinks.

For sure you will have a pizza night once a week because you will be too damn tired to cook. Of course this is alright. Pizza is awesome. The point here is to make the majority of your meals healthy ones.

Really pay attention to how you feel as you detox and energize your mind and body. You will notice higher energy levels, better sleep, calmer mind, and clearer thought. Use this progress to encourage you to continue with your program for healthy living.

Stock up

Stock up as much as you can before the baby is born. Preparation helps in a huge way. These are the things that you need to stock up on prior to the delivery date.

Prepared food

You can easily stock up food for at least two weeks, if not a month. The key here is to acquire or cook lots of healthy, prepared food. Freeze stuff in individual meal packages so that when you take them out of the freezer you do not have to thaw a bulk item in order to eat it.

Household supplies

Toilet paper, paper towels, water, personal care items, and laundry soap are all useful items to stock up on. Costco probably has the best deals on the first four items. You need laundry soap for adult laundry and soap for the baby's laundry. Buy lots of household supplies that have a long shelf life so you do not have to worry about this stuff for the first three months of the baby's life.

Diapers

It is a good idea to get some diapers. Not only will you need to put some diapers into your hospital go bag, you will basically be homebound for a few days after you bring your bundle home from the hospital and you need something for your baby to pee and poo into.

You also want to get some disposable wipes, these are much cheaper in bulk. Try to get ones which are reasonably chemical-free.

Newborn level diapers are really just used for the first couple of weeks, then you have to upgrade to the next level. Buy two weeks supply maximum of newborn nappies—newly born babies need about 15 changes per day, so you are looking at about 210 diapers. Also make sure that you buy Level "1" diapers so that you have them ready when "Newborn" diapers are too small.

Once you get all of this stuff, set up your battle station for diaper changing. There is much more detail on this in "The One-And-A-Half Minute Diaper Change" chapter later on.

Hospital go bag

You will need to pack a hospital "go bag" to supply you at the hospital during and after the labor and delivery. The basics include everything that you and your wife need to stay anywhere for 2-3 days, such as dental care, lotions, soaps, underwear, and a few changes of clothes. Your wife needs fewer changes of clothes since she will be in a hospital gown most of the time. It is also good to bring a robe if she gets sick of the hospital gown. Slippers are very useful in the hospital, so bring those. Pack a camera, or not if you want to rely upon your cell phone camera.

Bring entertainment like books or movies that are playable on a digital device. Bring your tablet. Definitely bring your chargers for your devices.

For baby, pack some newborn baby clothes like onesies, a shirt, and pants. A couple of swaddling blankets would be useful, although the hospital will probably give you some of these. Bring diapers for newborns as well. Babies do not pee or poo that much when they are just born, so you will probably just need 20 diapers for a two day stay. Also pack some disposable wipes.

You will need some mesh underwear, peri-pads, and a peri-bottle for after the delivery. "Peri"-stuff are used to take care of your wife's "down there" since the baby will have caused a lot of trauma going through the birth canal. Our hospital supplied these for us, so find out if your hospital does as well.

Newborn/infant car seat

You need one of these to take your kid home from the hospital. More details in the baby care section in the chapter on car seats.

Sleep

Stock up on sleep. OK, I know that you cannot actually store sleep within your body for use after the baby is born. I mean, bears and bumblebees can do it, why can't humans?

Even if you cannot physically stock up on slumber, enjoy the hell out of sleep while you can. Make sure your wife enjoys the hell out of sleep while she can. There are ways to get enough sleep with the baby around (see the chapter on the Sleep Rota), but it is so much easier to get some sleep while the bun is still in the oven.

Stocking up for the baby is kind of like stocking up for the upcoming zombie apocalypse, which is inevitably drawing nearer every day. You will have some trouble getting out of the house, so make sure that you have most of what you need already at hand (although unlike the future zombie Armageddon, you do not need melee weapons to take care of a baby). Think like the Boy Scouts, whose motto is "Be Prepared"—one of the reasons why the Boy Scouts will be among the last humans standing when the zombie hordes eventually overwhelm humanity.

Educate yourself

Education is the engine of all growth. Education is like changing the oil in your car—it makes your life run much smoother. Education cures the fear of anything, such as the fear of becoming a parent.

There are tons, and I mean literally tons of resources out there to prepare for your baby's arrival. Baby education can take many forms.

Courses

My wife and I took pre-natal, post-partum, and emergency courses before Victoria's birth. We took them at the hospital that we were going to have the birth at for all of our baby-related health care (this also happens to be my workplace, so this was extra convenient for me).

Pre-natal classes covered third trimester issues, what to expect when going into labor, when to go to the hospital, what natural and caesarian deliveries are like, and potential complications.

Post-partum classes went over how to take care of the baby for the first two weeks, breast feeding, and post-partum mental conditions. Emergency situations class dealt with hazards such as choking, anaphylaxis, and CPR.

Websites

Use with caution. You can take ten different websites on any baby topic, and five might say one thing and five might say the opposite. Use common sense and your doctor's advice when discerning the validity of any online theory on babies.

Health care professionals

We followed the advice of our health care professionals (obstetrician, breastfeeding clinician, pediatrician) when we had access to them. Batch your questions prior to meeting one of your care providers. There are no useless questions when it comes to the health of your wife and child.

Books

There are many excellent books on baby care; however, I got the most out of these two.

- "The Happiest Baby on the Block", by Harvey Karp. This is probably the best book out there on how to calm your crying baby, which means it is worth its weight in gold.
- "What to Expect When You're Expecting", by Heidi Murkoff, Arlene Eisenberg, and Sandee Hathaway. This is the classic book reviewing what happens from conception to taking care of a newborn. The first part of the book covers the basics of what to do when you find out you are pregnant. The second part reviews each month of

pregnancy. The last part of the book is a guide to post-partum care.

Read a lot! You can get the wisdom of thousands of authors through books.

Friends and family

Reach out to your inner circle for guidance on the care and feeding of your baby. Be selective on who you ask. You want to ask people who give positive encouragement and useful tips on how to make the transition to fatherhood in the best way possible.

Targeted education is absolutely one of the best things you can do to improve any area of your life. Educate yourself on how to be a great husband and father before the baby arrives. It is an excellent investment of your time.

Self-care post-partum

Congratulations! Your wife just gave birth and now you're a new dad. All the preparation had better come in handy!

Once the baby arrives, you need to stay healthy, rested, and happy in order to care for your wife and baby. Healthy because you need to do all the heavy lifting around the household while your wife is recuperating. Rested because you will need to work to provide for your family on top of all the domestic duties. Happy because the emotional well-being of your wife depends on it, and I am sure even newborn babies pick up on your mood.

You want to make sure that you are in a good state of being so that you can help your family—it is like putting the oxygen mask on yourself first before you help others in a mid-flight emergency. Fortunately you adopted a positive mental attitude before your wife gave birth. You also feel a sense of gratitude that you are able to create a new life. You now have faith in yourself that you can get the job done. You are physically fit because you put some work into your body in anticipation for your new role as a father. Your life is now optimized to make use of slivers of time that can be invested into your family. You have detoxified and energized your body with good habits.

So, we need to keep up with this baby thing, but now the focus moves from preparation to implementation.

Sleep rota

It is vital for new parents to get enough sleep. It is critical. Super-duper critical.

I hear about working dads who barely slept for the first few months of their baby's life and I wonder how it is possible. I know a guy who had to go to Emergency because he barely got enough sleep for the first three months of his son's life.

You and your wife absolutely need to sleep well in order to take care of the baby, earn money, and perform activities of daily living.

You guys need a sleep rota.

There a few considerations that you need to take into account to develop a sleep rota.

1. Is your wife breastfeeding? Breastfeeding requires a woman to extract milk from her breasts every 3-5 hours or else there is a risk of breast infection, called mastitis. Your sleep rota must take into account the fact that your wife needs to take milk out of her boobs at regular intervals.
2. Who is going to work? Is dad, mom, or both going to work?
3. How much sleep do you need to function well? Be honest with yourself on the minimum sleep that you need. Most adults can function well with 7.5 hours of sleep. Keep in mind that this is the

number of hours for continuous sleep. If you get interrupted sleep, you generally need more total hours of sleep.

My wife and I decided to breastfeed our baby, with formula as an occasional supplement. My wife has a great job where she can take a full year off work. I took two weeks off and then went back to work. This is a good scenario because it allowed my wife to focus on her physical recovery while I went out and earned the family's bacon. I shifted my work hours a little earlier to avoid rush hour as well as to get home earlier to spend some family time, which helped make our schedule work. I could survive on 6 to 6.5 hours of continuous sleep a night. My wife needs more, so we tried to optimize the number of hours of sleep that she got. Continuous sleep was impossible since my wife was breastfeeding, so we focused on maximizing her total hours of sleep instead.

This is how our rota went for the first two months of Victoria's life:

- I wake up around 6:00am and change the baby's diaper. This way my wife gets more precious time to sleep. If all's well I then hit the gym before work.
- I leave for work around 7:45am with my wife normally still asleep. When the baby is hungry she will wake up to breastfeed.
- During the day, my wife usually gets a couple of naps that total 2-3 hours of sleep.

- I get home around 5:30 and my wife and I try to eat together. If the baby needs attention, we eat in shifts.
- After dinner, I take over with the baby so that my wife can take a shower, do any self-care that she needs to do, and pump out any residual breast milk so that she can sleep.
- My wife goes to sleep around 9:00pm. I feed the baby with bottled breast milk, change diapers, and give her some education by reading to her and working on her visual focusing.
- I stay up until about 12:00am making sure the baby is well-fed, changed, and drowsy. She usually sleeps for another hour when my wife takes over.
- Throughout the night I sleep a solid 6 hours while my wife gets another 2 hours in between feedings.

Our sleep rota netted me 6 hours of uninterrupted sleep. My wife got 4 hours of uninterrupted sleep in the evenings, 2 hours during the night, and an additional 4 hours of naptime interspersed throughout the day totalling 10 hours sleep. This is a reasonable amount of sleep for us to operate healthily for the first two months of our baby's life.

On the weekend, my wife got to sleep as much as she needed while I filled in for baby care. I usually got a nap in as well. On the weekends we relaxed our schedule and just gave each other breaks when we needed them.

Keep in mind: your sleep rota will evolve as baby develops. Adapt well to the changes and you will be fine.

Things start to get way, way better around the two-to-three month mark. Some people may tell you of the "Hundred Day Miracle" when the baby starts sleeping through the night—this means sleeping six to eight hours at a stretch. At that point you can start relaxing your sleep rota and start living like normal human beings.

We were lucky as Victoria hit this mark early at two months. At that point, Victoria was sleeping almost exclusively at night, waking up a couple of times to feed for half an hour each time. My wife and I were able to change up our sleep rota into a much simpler routine:

- I wake up around 5 A.M. and work on projects and hit the gym.
- At 8:00 A.M. the girls wake up and I say bye before I go to work.
- After work, I come home, eat dinner, and play with my daughter.
- Both my wife and I go to sleep at around 10:30 A.M.
- Victoria wakes up once in the night around 4:30 A.M. for a feed then goes back to sleep.

This simpler sleep schedule netted me 6.5 hours of solid uninterrupted sleep. My wife got two sessions of continuous sleep each about 4-6 hours long, as well as naps throughout the day, totalling over 10 hours a day.

Several men that I know were forced to wake up by their wives during nighttime feedings. These men say that their wives made them wake up because it made things "fair". I have spoken with women who made their husbands endure the same sleep schedule as they do—they generally admit that it makes no sense why they wake their husbands at night whenever baby wakes up.

I suggest that it is pointless to have both parents awake and sleeping in synchrony. This is a misguided notion of fairness. It is far more efficient to split up tasks and schedule shifts so that both partners can get the rest they need. For most baby care activities, one person can handle it so shifts make sense. It is optimal for the other partner to catch a few zz's while baby care is covered. A simple sleep rota can ensure that both partners get enough sleep to function.

Sleep is absolutely critical and should be made a priority. A newborn's safety depends on parents being alert—can you navigate the stairs and furniture while carrying your baby on only 3 hours of broken sleep per day? You need to be rested so that your wife can depend on you emotionally and physically. You need sleep to continue to excel at your work so that you can pay for food and all that baby stuff. Crashing your car on the way to work because you did not get enough sleep does not help the family cause. Getting fired for mental lapses due to sleep deprivation does not help the family cause.

You can obviously adopt this advice to your specific situation if you, the dad, is staying at home and your wife is working. Basically both of you need to get enough sleep so that accidents don't happen. Think of a way to make that happen.

Getting enough sleep for you and your wife is the most important thing you can do to take care of yourselves. With enough sleep you will have the energy and mental sharpness to tackle the challenges of caring for a baby.

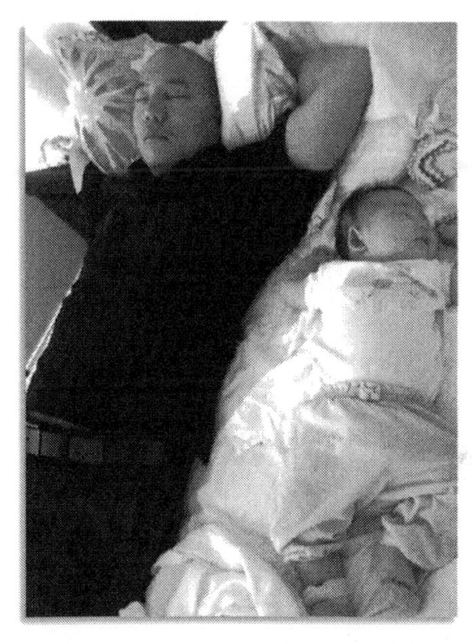

Get some sleep guys. It's totally necessary.

Work on projects

Even with a newborn baby around the house, you are going to have some downtime. Rather than catch up on your favorite TV shows, why don't you do some home improvement projects? Men need to use their brains to build things with their hands. It simply makes us happier people, especially in stressor situations like the transition into fatherhood.

It is amazing how much you can do at home with a newborn baby around. After my wife gave birth, I spent two weeks at home helping with baby care, but I also: mowed the lawn, installed three magnetic boards, put up some drapes in the sun room, installed outdoor lighting, built a bathroom shelf, cleaned out the garage, and repaired the grout in the kitchen floor.

Another one of the things that I did during the first few months of Victoria's life is to write this book. I basically snatched at slivers of time in between all the baby care and family obligations, and got it done.

Working on projects trains you to be optimal with your time. Now that you have a baby, time becomes a very valuable resource. The strange thing that happened to me after Victoria was born was that I got more done in my life. I fixed stuff around the house, I was incredibly productive at work, and I finished projects like this book. The same can happen for any new father with the right attitude.

Why not be productive as well as be a great father? It is good practice to maximize use of your time now that the baby has arrived.

Exercising with your baby

Can't make it to the gym for the first few weeks of your baby's life? Try some of these baby-plus-body-weight exercises. These motions do double duty: they keep you fit, and newborns freaking love being in motion. So, pump some iron and calm your baby with the following exercises.

These exercises require securing your baby in her car seat carrier.

Lawnmowers

Put your left foot forward into a lunge position. Place your left elbow on your left knee. Grab the carrier with your right arm and row backwards. Repeat for 8-12 repetitions (all of the following exercises can also be done with 8-12 reps). Repeat for the other side. This exercise works the latissimus dorsi and biceps.

Bicep curls

Stand with feet shoulder width apart. Pick up the baby carrier and curl your arm, flexing your bicep as you move through the motion. This exercise builds your biceps.

The following exercises require you to hold your baby in your arms.

Squats

Stand with your baby in your arms. Have your feet shoulder width apart. Slowly bend your knees and go into a squat. Raise yourself slowly into standing position. This exercise works the quadriceps and calf muscles.

Lunges

Again, stand with your baby with feet slightly narrower than shoulder width apart. Step back into a lunge and hold for two seconds. Step back into standing position. Do both legs. This exercises the hamstring muscles.

Horse-riding stance

Hold your baby in your arms. Place your feet at one-and-a-half shoulder width apart. Go into horse-riding stance like Gangnam Style. Bounce slowly up and down. This strengthens your abductor and adductor muscles as well as your glutes and abdominals.

Isotonic bicep hold

Cradle your baby in one of your arms. Use your other arm for stability. Hold until your arm starts to tire, then switch. This is another bicep exercise.

I found personally that Victoria loves the motion from these exercises, especially the up-and-down movements. It would often calm her down while giving me an exercise boost.

Use common sense with these moves. Do not move too fast as you do not want to hurt your baby. If your newborn hates it, she will let you know that you need to stop. Do not lift to muscle failure for safety reasons. Obviously, do not drop the baby like you drop the weights at the gym.

As your baby grows, more weight will be added so you will not plateau. The above exercises are a decent supplement to going to the gym; however, your primary exercise source should be the gym or a home exercise regimen.

Primary exercise

Bicep curls with your baby in the car seat works to get a decent pump, but you really need to keep up your primary exercise routine in order to function optimally. Hitting the gym is a new challenge with a baby around. Your time is no longer exclusively your own. As with all things important in life, if you do not have time for a thing, you make time for that thing.

My gym is a 5 minute jog from my house, so it has always been convenient for me to go. When my baby arrived, I had to figure out a time when I could regularly hit the gym. That time used to be "anytime", but after the baby I always went at 6:30 A.M. At this time, my wife and baby were usually fast asleep. Also at this time I was able to go to the gym before work. I never used to work out in the morning, but I got used to it and now I even like it. A morning workout gets blood flowing throughout the body and brain. It is a great way to start a productive day.

Another excellent way to keep fit is to just work out at home. I used to exclusively work out at home to workout videos. There are some seriously great home fitness systems out there. Select the system that is right for you, something that matches your fitness level and available workout duration. The best thing about working out at home is that there is no travel time to get to the gym.

Keep in mind the underlying reasons for making your body strong: your body needs to function properly to handle the physical and mental load of caring for a baby in addition to your regular duties as the man of the house. If you maintain your body, taking care of a baby gets much easier.

Be the rock

"And when the machine breaks down, we break down. And I ain't gonna allow that!" –Sgt. Barnes, Platoon (1986)

It goes without saying that if you break down, things will turn into a pretty hot mess. But that ain't gonna happen to you.

Being a man means to be the rock for your wife and child during the first few months after birth. You need to lead during this time. You need to take on the heavy lifting during this time. This is the part in the hockey game where your team needs you to step up to get that clutch goal.

It can potentially be a difficult time for everyone, but as long as you are maintaining yourself physically, emotionally, and mentally, things ought to go much more smoothly. The previous chapters outline a guide for yourself to meet one of life's big challenges and win. Follow this guide and you will not only survive, but you can also thrive.

Comport yourself well around your new family, enjoy the ride, but most importantly, be the rock that your family gets built upon.

Self-care recap

Taking care of yourself is essential to being a great father and husband. A man with a well-maintained mind and body is far better equipped to handle the rigors of fatherhood and marriage than a man who has not done any work on himself.

This part of the book covered the following:

- Adopt a positive mental attitude. Make sure that you always have gratitude and faith in yourself that you can get the job done. Figure out that you really want to be a great dad and get to work.
- Bring some order to your life. Tune the machine that is your body with exercise and great food. Optimize as many facets of your life as you can.
- Stock up like you are about to face the zombie apocalypse.
- Educate yourself. It is the cure to fear and elicits action to make the transition to fatherhood that much easier.
- Sleep rotas. Totally necessary. Make sure you and your wife get enough sleep.
- Work on projects at home because a man needs to build things with his hands to be happy.
- Get your exercise after the baby arrives. You will need to be fit and trim to take care of your noisy and occasionally very dirty little offspring.

Now let us focus on the most important member of your team: your wife.

Part 2

Wife-care:

Happy wife, happy (post-baby) life!

Happy wife, happy (post-baby) life

It is largely up to you to be the rock for your wife while she is recovering from the birth. The happier, well-rested, and calm your wife is, the happier, well-rested, and calm you are as well. And the baby gets care from two happy, well-rested, and calm adults, making her happy, well-rested, and calm—relatively speaking, as far as babies go. It is a virtuous cycle. They say "happy wife, happy life". This totally holds true when a baby comes along.

Marriage needs team work. When one of the players is down due to injury or fatigue, the other steps up the effort for the team. After birth, your wife is essentially on the injury list for a few weeks. She will need all the help she can get to recover while at the same time taking care of the new addition in the family. It is up to you to step up your effort so that your household runs smoothly, your wife can get healthy, and your baby gets the best care.

Your wife's state before and after birth

Unless your wife is the Rambo-type, just before birth she may be scared. She has gone to the dark corners of the internet and learned about episiotomies, defecation during birth, bleeding, tearing, and how bloody long labor is for a first child. She probably has pregnant friends with whom she regularly talks about this stuff, and they all collectively freak each other out.

My wife is a strong independent woman. She has lived in and traveled to several countries around the world. Her job requires her to work with politicians, public figures, foreign dignitaries, and even movie directors. She is certainly no shrinking violet. Yet she still had a lot of trepidation as we approached the birth of our daughter.

I had to do a lot of work to keep up my wife's confidence that she could get the job done. I assured my wife that I would be there every step of the way. I kept her off websites and forums where women scare each other about childbirth. I tried to encourage her to not collectively freak out with her five other friends who were giving birth at around the same time. The cure to fear is action. Once things move into action, there will be no time for fear.

Your wife may be feeling that she is approaching the end of her former life as a single person. Even being married without children is like being "single" in that she does not have to take care of a helpless little human being for God knows how long. She will want to go to the movies one last time, eat a steak dinner one last time, go out with friends for one last time… well, she will think it is the last time she does these things. Just keep reminding her that this is just another phase in life and that she has much to look forward to in her new life as a mother. And remind her that she will of course go to the movies again, eat steak dinners again, and go out with her friends again.

Be understanding and kind. This whole baby thing will affect her *waaaaay* more than it will affect you. It is good to be a guy—that is for sure. But just because you do not have to go through childbirth does not mean that you are off the hook. Support the hell out of your wife before, during, and after the baby's delivery.

After your wife gives birth, you need to be the rock-steady man in her life to guide her through a tough period. Again, it is important to realize that what your wife is going through is far more life-changing than anything that you will go through. Consider all of the changes that she will go through in a short span of time:

- She will either have passed a large object through her birth canal or a doctor will cut out a living being from her abdomen like that movie *Alien*. Both cause an incredible amount of trauma.
- Her social life will have dramatically changed—she will be mourning her former life.

- She will have this totally helpless and often very cranky baby to nurture.
- Her body will have changed a lot—think stretch marks, rock-hard boobs, joint pain, etc.
- Nothing fits anymore.
- She will be physically and mentally weak for months.
- Her hormones will be wreaking havoc on her systems, specifically the hormones relaxin and oxytocin.

This sounds like the Navy SEAL orientation known as "Hell Week", except longer and way harder. Just put yourself in her shoes and realize that (a) it's good to be a guy and (b) you owe her big time.

It bears repeating: support the hell out of your wife physically and emotionally.

Provide or acquire support for the first two weeks

It is very important to line up continuous support for your wife for at least two weeks post-partum. This could take many forms. I am fortunate to have work where I can flexibly take time off based on when the baby is born. Many of you also have this flexibility. If you can schedule two weeks of vacation that starts with the day your wife goes into labor, this is the best scenario. You can be at home with your new family for the first two weeks of your baby's life. Bonding with the baby is as important for a father as it is for a mother, so this time together is absolute gold.

I loved having my two weeks off to take care of my new family. I could focus on making sure that my wife and my baby had everything that they needed. I could bond with my newborn daughter. As mentioned earlier, I also got to do a number of projects that made my house more livable and more optimized for baby care.

There are also people who offer their services to new moms and dads to help run the household for that first critical period of time. You can find and book these services ahead of time. It is kind of like having a short-term nanny.

Family can also help out to varying degrees. When you bring baby home, you will realize how valuable home-cooked prepared food is, since you will have little time to cook yourself. Ask family to bring prepared food, not flowers or other gifts, when they visit you for the first little while. Also, if you can book family members to help out around the house after the baby is born, this is another great option for support.

Be there for emotional support

It is pretty much guaranteed that your wife will break down in tears sometime during the first couple of weeks. It makes total sense when you force your man brain to think about what is going on.

Your wife just got her butt kicked giving birth. Her hormones are still raging inside her and causing havoc with her physical systems. Her insides have been stretched to hell and in some places torn and stitched back together. She is weak from the ordeal and cannot do much for herself, yet she has the task of caring for a helpless infant that *has to be carried out*.

Her body has changed. There are stretch marks across her abdomen and this weird black line running up and down the middle of her belly. Her abs are flab. Her uterus has not shrunk yet so she still feels like she is semi-pregnant.

Her former life is essentially over. She will be in mourning. No more lattes with friends without having to worry about her baby. No more shopping trips for clothes to make her look and feel good. No more freedom of the single life. No more getting destroyed at pubs until 3AM (ok, maybe I'm talking about me there).

All of these things combine to overwhelm your wife's emotions. Your wife will likely break down in tears a few times.

Your job is to love and support your wife to get her through this difficult time. Listen to her. Empathize with her. Keep telling her that things will definitely get better, and soon. Women are different from men. When women are emotionally distraught, they want understanding, compassion, and connection. When men are in trouble, they want solutions to problems. Do not give her solutions to problems, it is not what she wants. What she wants is her man to offer a shoulder to cry on.

This feeling of temporary malaise is called the "baby blues". This is apparently extremely common—all of my wife's friends got this to some degree. For us, the worst of it was over in less than a week. If things get more serious, you might be seeing symptoms of post-partum depression. If your wife is showing signs of flat-out depression, seek professional help from your general practitioner.

After the first two weeks, your wife's energy will start to ramp up again. Her insides will have largely recovered from the trauma of birth at around six weeks. Stretch marks and the weird black belly line will start fading away. By three months, the emotional roller coaster will have slowed down. Abs will get tighter with exercise over the next year. And her friends will still be there, lattes are still there, and shopping is still there (although you will both be spending much more time at Baby Gap than Nordstrom, for obvious reasons!).

It is way different for a man to adjust to life after a baby is born. There are no body changes or hormonal disruption. There is no demanding baby trying to extract life blood from you. You still have freedom of mobility. So it is up to you to help your wife through the first few weeks and months. Be her shoulder to cry on when her emotions start overwhelming her.

Be there for physical support

You need to physically support your wife after birth, quite literally. Birth kicks the crap out of a woman's physical systems. Her hormones wreak havoc, her uterus shrinks rapidly, her insides are pummeled, and her energy is sapped.

During and after birth, the hormone relaxin courses through a woman's body. This hormone is produced by the placenta and ovaries. Its purpose is to relax the ligaments in the pelvis and soften the cervix so that the baby can pass through the birth canal. Once the baby is delivered this hormone is still pumping through the body. This causes a kind of post-partum arthritis where the joints everywhere feel lax and painful. Nature is a bitch when it comes to relaxin: just when a woman needs to be lugging around a 6-10 pound newborn baby, her musculoskeletal system goes weak on her.

After birth, there are all sorts of tissue damage that your wife needs to get over. Think of the hardest weight lifting workout you have ever performed and how much it hurt to recover from it in the days afterward. Your wife basically will experience this times ten. Your wife will have gotten her ass kicked to Mars and back again. She will be tired. It will be difficult for her to walk around.

The commonly quoted recovery duration for a mother who just gave birth is six weeks. Six weeks is enough time for the majority of healing to occur; however, joint pain, muscle soreness, and fatigue may continue for a few more weeks. So, there is a significant amount of time between the birth and your wife's recovery where there is a lot of slack to be picked up when it comes to the physical work needed to take care of the baby and run the household.

Fortunately, you are a strong, fit man who has been working on his physical self for weeks and months before the birth. You have worked on your inner self and gained appreciation for the miracle of having a child. This is where the investments in your physical fitness and inner mental game start to pay off dividends.

These are the things a man needs to do to physically support his recovering wife during the first couple of months:

Carry the baby

Your baby will need to be held a lot. It calms her down. For nine months, your baby was nestled warm and snug inside a comforting bath of amniotic fluid and her own urine (seriously, urine—look it up). Your baby is used to being carried 24 hours a day, 7 days a week. It is impossible to spoil a baby with too much holding. In fact, newborns absolutely love being held. Take on the bulk of holding your baby, especially in the first six weeks of your wife's recovery. Your wife's joints will be too weak and sore to deal with too many weight bearing tasks.

Do all the chores

Yes, all of them. Laundry, dishes, food prep, vacuuming, and cleaning. Your wife needs rest, heavy lifting around the house might hinder her recovery. If you cannot afford the time but can afford the money, temporarily hire a housekeeper to help you out now and then.

Bring stuff to her

Your wife will need stuff brought to her like water, food, books, her cell phone, and her baby. When she asks, get up and get what she needs.

Change all the diapers

Your baby will pee and poo very frequently during the first month—as much as 15 times a day. Pick the baby up and change her diaper. Your wife will have enough on her plate just breastfeeding.

Be someone to lean on

Help her into the car. Hold her arm when she is walking around. Be there to physically support her.

Handling most of the physical chores for the first few weeks after the baby is born should not be confused with you taking on the role of the family doormat.

This is absolutely not the case. In any marriage, there should be a synergistic sharing of household duties done in the spirit of teamwork. In the time after your baby is born, your wife's primary physical responsibility is to feed the baby and to recover. Your physical responsibility is quite literally everything else.

This will change over time as your wife recovers and your baby develops, such that the physically demanding household chores get rebalanced.

Protect your wife from her maternal instinct

Your wife will be hit by a force of nature that she cannot explain. She will not realize the strength of its effect on her. Due to this force, she will be compelled to follow it even at a detriment to her own health.

This force is the maternal instinct.

The maternal instinct is that force of nature that compels a mother to defend and nurture her offspring. The maternal instinct is critical for a baby's well-being. If a new mother did not feel so strongly to protect and nurture her child none of us would be here. It drives a woman to focus all of her attention and energies towards this helpless, noisy, and occasionally dirty little being.

The maternal instinct is driven primarily by the hormone oxytocin. Oxytocin floods a woman's body during and after birth. It is the hormone that elicits uterine contractions during labor. It also works on how close she feels with the person who is around when the hormone is released into her system. Oxytocin is the bonding hormone. Oxytocin is nature's Love Potion No. 9. If you could bottle up oxytocin, oxycodone would go out of business. Oxytocin is released during breastfeeding and cuddling, so every time a mother breastfeeds she feels a maternal bond with her child.

This is an overwhelming instinct, but it is also a stealthy instinct. Your wife might not even know how powerful this force impacts her actions. It might get to the point where a new mother neglects to take care of herself because she is so strongly focused on her child. This is where you need to step in. Watch your wife to see signs that she is not eating right, not getting outside enough, not caring for her injuries after birth, and not taking whatever post-partum vitamins and minerals her doctor recommends.

Just after our daughter was born, my wife was very focused on the responsibility of taking care of our small newborn baby, so she missed taking her iron pills for a few days (in her case, our doctor recommended iron pills). This led to extreme exhaustion to the point where she could barely get up out of bed. It was scary when this happened as she nearly fainted on me. I bought a pound of beef for her to eat and she started taking her pills again. After that episode I made sure I was more vigilant.

The maternal instinct is clearly important for a mother to care for her child; however, it definitely does not help if it overrides the self-preservation instinct. If a mother is incapacitated this is obviously not good for the baby. When my wife became iron-deficient this impeded her ability to take care of Victoria. Think of the directive that flight attendants give on airplanes to put the oxygen mask on yourself before you help others in an air pressure loss scenario. Your wife needs to be healthy in order for your baby to be healthy.

Keep an eye on your wife to make sure she keeps up her self-care of her post-partum wounds. A woman's "down there" is a mess after birth. Sitz baths with Epsom salts may help soothe the wounds (ask your doctor for advice on this). Her joints are sore and weak from the hormone relaxin, so make sure she does not strain herself physically. She is also totally exhausted from the ordeal. Analgesic drugs may still course through her body from the epidural application or general anesthetic. Your wife will need to do a lot of self-care to recover from the birth. Make sure she takes the steps to take care of herself.

Sleep

Earlier on, I touched on the subject of sleep. Sleep is incredibly important for the human body to function well. If you or your wife is not getting enough sleep, the quality of care for your baby is compromised. Safety is also a major concern, since sleep-deprived parents cannot hold onto squirming babies very well.

Sleep is a difficult resource to acquire especially in the first 2-3 months of your baby's life. Although newborn babies sleep around 16 hours a day the duration of their sleeping periods are very short, typically between 1-3 hours. Having to adapt to this fractured sleeping pattern is ruinous to an adult's sleep hygiene. The brunt of sleep-deprivation is generally borne by the mother, especially if she is breastfeeding.

Maintaining a sleep rota for the first 2-3 months can significantly alleviate your wife's sleep deprivation. There are many ways to arrange this, but the idea is to maximize (a) continuous sleep hours and (b) total sleep hours for you and your wife. A sleep rota can morph over time as the baby starts sleeping through the night. Refer to the earlier chapter on sleep rotas for more details.

It is important to ensure that your wife gets enough sleep. As discussed in the previous chapter, a new mother's maternal instinct can get in the way of doing the right things for her health. If you have the baby covered for a few hours, really make sure your wife hits the sack for some well-deserved zzz's even if she claims she does not need it. Monitor her sleep hours. Make sure that she gets at least eight hours of sleep a day (preferably much more) even if it is broken up.

The more rested your wife is the better she will be able to function and the happier your family will be. I cannot stress this enough—both of you need to get enough sleep!

Going outside is restorative to mind and body

One of the most restorative things that a person can do for one's mood is to go outside. This certainly holds true for women who just gave birth. Our pediatrician advised my wife to get out often as it is great for her mood and staves off depression. Going outside and listening to rustling leaves, feeling the sunshine on the skin, and breathing clean air is an excellent break from putting up with a screaming baby in an enclosed space.

We live in a nice neighborhood with lots of trees and parks, and our own backyard is an oasis of calm. My wife totally understood that it is curative to be outside after giving birth. She normally loves going outside. During our dating life and our first year of marriage (before the baby) she was always going out to meet with friends, volunteer, work out, or organize an event. After birth, the kicker was that she absolutely hated the idea of being outside and resisted it with every fiber of her being.

I am not sure about the psychology or physiology behind this resistance, but I can take some educated guesses. After birth, a woman is physically and mentally exhausted. Going outside might represent a huge mental hurdle when in this condition. There are hormones zipping through her body that confuse the hell out of a woman who just gave birth, so perhaps the instinct is to stay safely inside the nest. The "baby blues" may cause a woman to further turtle into her shell.

Whatever the reason, I am absolutely convinced that going outside is a great break for women caring for their newborns. Each time my wife went outside for a walk around the block or even just a few minutes in the backyard her mood lightened up. And when her mood lightened up, the baby sensed it and was calmer. And when my wife's mood improved I was happier and more energetic, so I was a better caregiver and husband. After three weeks, my wife was regularly going outside on walks, sometimes alone and sometimes with the baby.

One way you can help get her outside is to assemble, test out, and deploy your outdoor baby carrier system. This may be a stroller equipped with a bassinet or a baby sling (these are good only if your baby has grown large enough—see manufacturer's guidelines for safe use with newborn babies). If you can take the baby with you on walks, this will encourage your wife to get outside.

Once she gets used to being outside, your wife will start to love going out again. Try to get to this point as soon as possible. Going outside is one of the simplest ways to care for your wife's well-being after she gets her ass kicked by giving birth.

Get her family and friends over

Your wife will need to lean on her support network in the weeks after birth. She will have to by and large stay at home for weeks to recover, so company will be quite welcome. Get her family and friends to come over, and often. They will bring useful gifts, flowers, and good cheer to your glum significant other. It will help a lot.

When people come over, they might ask what they can bring over to help. The best answer is **PREPARED FOOD**. You and your wife will be very busy taking care of the little one, leaving not much time to cook.

When family and friends come over, this will provide a much needed break for your wife from the baby. Others will want to hold your baby and give her lots of attention. It is a good idea to let this happen.

Also, consider that your wife would want to talk with actual adults from time to time rather than a mute newborn. Although you, as her husband, can provide some mature conversation, you will be quite busy with taking care of the baby and also running the whole household. Welcome guests to your home, and often. It really helps.

Be at home as much as possible

This one should be obvious. For at least the next six months, no bar hopping for you.

Obvious, but still a shock to the system. Guess what guys: your time no longer belongs exclusively to you. And no, your time does not belong to your wife (unless your wife is a ball-busting slave-driver and you like the punishment, but for the sake of argument let's just say that you married well and your wife is wonderful). Your time now belongs to your new family, with the neediest member being your newborn child.

The responsible thing is to now be at home whenever you possibly could. Trim work hours, multi-task shopping errands, and be a cheap bastard with your time so that you can spend it with your new family.

Of course, this is also a very fun and rewarding time. Oxytocin works on men as well—it is generated by cuddling with your baby—so you will feel a bond towards your baby that grows over time. Seeing all the developmental changes as they happen is very rewarding as a parent. You want to bond with your child at the earliest stages as it will become very difficult to make up for a lack of bonding time once your kid becomes a toddler (this is currently a major problem with a couple of our friends where the toddler rejects or is distant with the dad). Once you get over the hump and adjust to your new life as a parent, you will want to be at home as much as possible.

You want to start this thing off right. In her book *The Top Five Regrets of the Dying*, Bronnie Ware, a palliative care nurse, says that male patients very often regret doing things that take time away from their families. Don't even start down that path. As soon as you have your first kid, you are a family man. Feel blessed and be the best damn dad you can possibly be.

Hit on your wife to make her feel attractive

Your wife will feel the opposite of sexy after she gives birth. Not hard to figure that out. Her body will be bruised and torn apart from the trauma of birth. Her joints will hurt like hell from all the relaxin hormone pumping through her body. The baby blues will kick in. Her skin will bear stretch marks. She is in her P.J.'s all day.

So hit on your wife every now and then. It will affirm in her mind that you still think she is attractive. It will affirm in your mind that you still think she is attractive. Romance is hard to stop and start up again, so keep the engine humming at all times.

You can do this in a kind and loving way. Simply kissing her at random times can go a long way. Small gifts of kindness are amazing during this time, like taking care of the baby while your wife goes out for tea with her friends. You can hit on her in dirty ways. Bite your lip and ogle inappropriately at her while she is breastfeeding. Make suggestive comments to her in front of the baby. When milk starts flooding her boobs they will get rock hard and perky which is genuinely kind of hot—make sure she knows you noticed. I liked to waltz with my wife to the music coming from the baby's electronic mobile—my wife cracked up when I did that. Try to lay on the cheese and make her laugh.

Never say something like "even though you have stretch marks, you're still hot", unless you want to get face-planted on a hot stove element.

Just use your head and make her feel pretty. She'll appreciate it.

Have your wife go on field trips without the baby

Want to know what is the best gift you can give your wife in the first few months after the baby arrives? Take care of the baby while she goes out and *does whatever the hell she wants*.

This requires timing and forethought. You need to consider the following timed elements and schedule your wife's field trips accordingly:

1. Your baby needs to be fed at regular intervals, depending on her stage of development. Your wife should go out at the start of one of these intervals.
2. Your wife's breasts need to be emptied of milk at regular intervals. In the first month-and-a-half, her breasts can fill up like crazy and are not synchronized with the baby's hunger. Later on, milk production and the baby's stomach will synchronize. Your wife should go out with her breasts emptied.
3. Babies eventually develop a sleep schedule. It is preferable (but not necessary) to time your wife's outing during baby's naptime.

Your wife will really appreciate that you take a long baby care shift so that she can go out. Whenever I take on the baby care duties for one of my wife's field trips, she does a double fist pump and screams "FREEDOM!!!" like Braveheart before bolting out the door.

I mean, think about it. Your wife works 24/7 feeding and caring for a baby who cannot socially interact with her at an adult level. It is all baby talk all the time. I would go crazy if I did not have the occasional outlet.

Encourage her to go out with her girlfriends. Suggest that she go to a café and read a book. Or drop her off at the mall so that she can go shopping for herself (ban baby stores on these outings). Have her pick up her work out routine again. My wife loves Pilates, so I encouraged her to start up again at the local community center.

Don't worry about your wife never coming back from these field trips after tasting sweet freedom. The maternal instinct will pull her back every time.

Wife-care recap

Your wife needs to be healthy and happy for your family to be healthy and happy. As your wife has just gone through the crazy trauma of birth, it is up to you to lead your new family. To recap the wife-care part of this book:

- Happy wife, happy (post-baby) life: make sure that your wife is taken care of as much as you can. Your wife's state before and after birth is full of emotional and physical trials, especially for the first child.
- Provide or acquire support for the first two weeks. Either take time off work, ask family members for help, or hire someone.
- Be there for emotional and physical support. Your wife has been through the wringer of birth so make sure that you are there for her.
- Protect your wife from her maternal instinct. Make sure she takes care of herself as she will have all of her focus on the baby.
- Sleep. So important. Keep track of your wife's sleep and arrange for her to get more as needed.
- Kick her outside even if she hates the idea. Outside air is refreshing and invigorating.
- Get her family and friends over to help out.
- No going out for a while—be at home as much as possible.
- Hit on your wife to make her feel attractive.

- Have your wife go on field trips without the baby. It is the best gift that you can give to her.

Now that we've covered how to take care of yourself and how to take care of your wife, let us get into the most important section of this book: how to take care of your baby.

Part 3

Baby-care:
All Systems Are Go!

Systems are everything

When it comes to baby care, systems are everything. When you are changing 15 diapers a day, feeding 8-10 times per day, calming fussiness, bathing, and settling your child to sleep, you need to be able to do each thing efficiently. Having an optimized system for each operation will make the overall enterprise of baby-rearing much easier.

Take something as simple as diaper changing. An un-optimized diaper changing area might take 4 minutes per change; a well-optimized diaper-changing battle station will process a diaper change once every 1.5 minutes (more on that in the diapers chapter). Over the course of a day (about 15 changes for a newborn baby), you are talking about 1 hour total time using an un-optimized system and only 22.5 minutes using an optimized system.

Apply optimized systems over everything that you do for baby and you will actually find that you have spare time throughout the day to do crazy projects like write a baby how-to book for new dads.

This last part of the book on baby care is essentially about optimizing your systems for baby care so that your infant gets quality parenting efficiently and easily.

The one-and-a-half minute diaper change

Diapers are seriously not even close to the hardest thing about having a baby. Changing diapers is the easiest thing in the world, and I will tell you why:

1. It is quick and easy to do with an optimized system.
2. Babies stop crying once you change them. They totally love it.

Diaper changes take approximately 1.5 minutes, as long as your diaper changing system is optimized. Over 15 diaper changes a day, this only adds up to 22.5 minutes per day. Compared to feeding and calming, this is a piece of cake.

You need to have the baby wearing clothing that makes it easy to access her diapers. Loose pants and onesies that button up at the diaper level are good options. Pick the best, most diaper-accessible clothing based on the seasons.

Have a battle station well-stocked with everything that you need to change diapers. Once you have everything optimized, yes, diapers take 1.5 minutes to change.

The best thing about changing your kid's diapers is that they often calm right down once you do. They usually have a "dirty diaper cry" and a "dirty diaper face" that will clue you in as to the state of her undies. You will definitely get familiar with these cues in the first couple of weeks!

What you need at your diaper station:

- Two dozen diapers ready to go and at arm's length
- Another two dozen diapers in a storage location close by
- A changing pad with linen on top
- A half dozen baby towels close at hand
- Baby wet naps
- A pile of clean baby rags
- Barrier cream (we use cream with zinc oxide in it, it soothes diaper rash)
- Baby-safe moisturizer
- Diaper pail with a foot pedal that operates the lid
- Generic garbage bin
- Laundry hamper within shooting distance

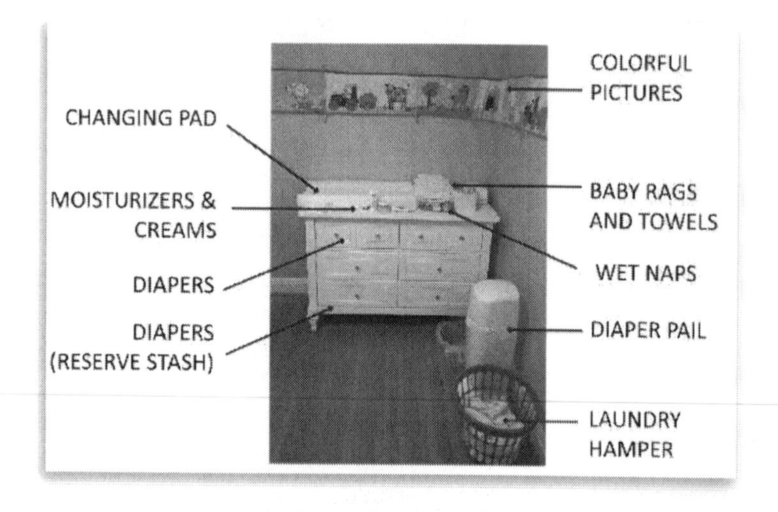

Our diaper-changing battle station.

The kind of diaper that you buy is key to your success. We tried many brand name products, and also some weird naturopathic diapers. By far, we liked diapers with an indicator strip. When dry, the strip is yellow. When wet, it is blue. So when baby's bawling her head off, it is a very quick check to see if the diaper is the problem.

We never considered linen diapers because they sounded like too much maintenance. I understand that there are environmental reasons for using these, so of course go with your conscience. I figure that disposable diapers are not so bad to use because my city composts all diapers. My baby's output is probably feeding a tree right now.

The one-and-a-half minute diaper change goes as follows:

1. Place baby on changing table. (5 seconds)
2. Grab a new diaper and place it beside the baby. (5 seconds)
3. Strip off pants or unbutton onesie to access the diaper area. (5 seconds)
4. Unstrap the dirty diaper, mopping up as much as possible with the clean parts of the diaper (usually the front part of the diaper that covers the belly). (15 seconds)
5. Grab a wet nap and wipe up the mess. For girls, be careful not to contaminate her pee hole with stuff from the poo hole. (20 seconds)
6. Roll up the dirty diaper with the dirty wipes inside it and set it aside or shoot it into the diaper pail if within arm's length. (5 seconds)
7. Put some barrier cream onto your baby's butt. (5 seconds)
8. Grab the new diaper and put it on. Ensure that the diaper rides high up the back so that no mess leaks out. (20 seconds)
9. Put the pants back on or re-button the onesie. (10 seconds)

Believe me, all guys get really good at this really fast. Don't bother trying to set speed records for this kind of thing, you want to be safe and not make your baby uncomfortable. The point I am trying to make is that diaper changes really do not take that long and are really easy to do as long as you have the right tools.

Diaper resizing will occur from time to time. When poo breaches the diaper lining, then it is obviously time to increase the size of the diaper. This can happen in an orderly fashion or it can happen catastrophically. When it happens in an orderly manner, you will notice that the lining of the diaper (i.e. the last barrier of defense before the poo escapes) will start to stain with poo, and perhaps there is some spotting on the baby's clothing as well.

A catastrophic breach is an event where the lining gives way completely and soaks the baby's clothes, the crib, blankets, floor, and you with poo. Our first resizing (from newborn to Level 1) was triggered by a catastrophic breach. Victoria was in her crib at the time and basically soaked all of her bedding. Complete chaos!

Poo

Now that we talked about diapers, let's talk about poo.

In your pre-baby life, poo has not been an important part of your everyday conversations. As a new dad, you are going to be talking about poo all the time. This is because your baby will be defecating a half-dozen times a day—usually in a diaper, but sometimes in unexpected and unwanted places.

Every parent has a gross poo story. It is time to discover yours.

The first poo that comes out of your baby is called meconium. This is the first poo that comes out of the baby after birth. It is black/green, sticky, and hard to clean off. After 3 or 4 days, the poo morphs into this brown, green, and/or yellow mess. Around day 5, your baby's poo will look dark yellow, soft, and seedy.

Now, this all sounds a little disgusting, and it is, but not as much as you would think. A newborn baby's poo does not really smell that bad and does not really look like what comes out of adults, so you can disassociate from the grossness a little bit. Baby poo smells faintly like that pervasive "baby smell". Basically, not that bad. When a baby starts eating solid food (for us that was around six months), the poo morphs into something closer to adult poo—and definitely smells like adult poo, too!

Most of the baby's poo will get into the diaper; however, there is that 1% that ends up, well, not in the diaper. When a baby outgrows her diaper, you will know because poo will leak and it will be a chaotic mess wherever this happens to occur. Big leaks can also happen if the diaper is not correctly hiked far enough up your baby's backside, or the diaper's liner does not adequately cover the catchment zone. Babies also will poo anywhere, anytime, including while you are changing her which can create a really messy situation.

One time when my wife was changing diapers, Victoria let spew a jetstream of poo onto the floor, the changing table, and my wife's bathrobe. **Projectile poo.** It was utter chaos for half an hour having to deal with this. But still really funny! Mostly funny because it hit my wife and not me.

When poo happens, you really just have to deal with it. A good way to clean poo off of fabric is by soaking it in water with some added baking soda for a few hours, and then running it in the wash. Use cold water for the soak and for the wash. It is a good idea to have a basin on hand dedicated to soaking poo-stained clothing and linens. As a detergent, I use Nellie's All-Natural Baby Laundry. It is a baking soda-based detergent that is very mild and baby-safe. With the soak-and-wash technique, most of the poo should come off.

Get used to touching poo directly with your hands. You may even accidentally get it in your mouth. You may well be covered with the stuff from time to time. It is going to happen so just deal with it early on. If you want to dive right in, just place your hand in a soiled diaper and force yourself to hold it there for 30 seconds. It will get you used to the grossness of it.

Fortunately, poo takes the form of the yellow-seedy phase for the majority of the first three months—this stuff is easy to clean off and does not smell too bad.

When a baby poos, it can be explosive. It sounds like the largest, rudest fart you ever heard followed quickly by a gross squelching sound. One time when we were in church with Victoria, she defecated so loud that people several pews around us were searching around for the culprit. Whenever this sort of thing happens, just blame the baby.

No matter what you do, don't drop the baby

Obviously, don't drop the baby. Like, seriously, seriously, **don't drop the baby**. There are plenty of reasons to avoid this—again, *duh*, but let's review a few of these anyway.

There are two soft spots in the skull of a newborn baby called fontanelles. There is one in the front of the head and a smaller one in the back. If you look closely, you can see these soft spots pulsate with the baby's heartbeat. Fontanelles are there because they allow the skull to be flexible enough to deform as the baby's head passes through the birth canal. Although the brain is covered by a tough membrane called the dura mater (literally means "tough mother" in Latin), there is basically no hard skull bone protecting some parts of the baby's brain for the first 2-4 months. You definitely do not want the baby's head to experience any impact, especially for a newborn baby with soft spots in the skull.

If you drop the baby and she seems hurt, you will have to spend a panic-stricken several hours at the emergency ward to ensure that everything is ok. You will also endure a life-time of guilt and worry that you dropped your kid when she was a baby. You will be that guy who dropped his baby. If your kid gets a C- in eleventh grade English, you might be thinking that she might have gotten an A if you did not drop her on the head as a baby. These concerns are all things to avoid.

We live in an age where someone will call Child Protection Services if kids are seen playing in their own backyard without a parent immediately visible, or if there is bruising seen on a kid's arm or leg. My wife, my baby, and I are Korean—one marker on many Asian babies is a black-blue spot in the lower back called a "Mongolian spot". We were told to take a picture right after birth to better document what this spot was, since some daycare workers may report child abuse from spanking too hard if they saw this very common birthmark. So if you drop the baby and she has some visible injury, then this could mean trouble from well-meaning but disruptive do-gooders who may report you to the cops.

You really do not want to drop the baby because she is precious. It is vital that you prevent any physical or mental damage when she is at such a young age.

Although accidents can happen, there are several things you can do to drastically reduce the risk of dropping your baby.

The most important thing that you can do is instill a safety culture in your household when you bring your baby home from the hospital.

Have a conversation with your wife about safety. Brainstorm all the ways that you can avoid dropping the baby in your home. These are some of the things that my wife and I do to reduce risk:

- When navigating the stairs with the baby, we adopt a one-armed football hold with our daughter and use the other hand to hold the rail.
- Make sure we are both getting enough sleep so that we don't pass out in a chair and drop the baby or stumble over something because we are sleep-deprived.
- Ensure the floor is clear of trip- or slip-hazards.
- When we are transferring Victoria between each other, we pause mid-transfer to ensure that the other person is securely holding the baby.

Once your safety rules are in place, try to make that safety culture flourish. Make sure you and your wife are making it a priority.

Use your man brain to ensure bad things don't happen. The primitive, lizard part of the male brain protects you from stuff that will lead to complete disaster. The man brain ensures that men never leave the house without the Holy Trinity: wallet, keys, and cell phone. The man brain also never allows the Holy Trinity to get lost or stolen when going about town. The man brain always has men disengage the parking brake while driving. Whatever a man does for work (forklift driver, heart surgeon, master craftsman, whatever) the man brain focuses on the task at hand and avoids disaster. Apply your man brain to ensure that you never, ever drop the baby.

Car seats, strollers, and slings

Baby transportation needs to be worked out before the birth. There are two basic aspects of transportation that you need to resolve: transport by car and transport on foot.

You need to own an infant car seat to take your baby home from the hospital safely as well as to generally transport your child in your car. My sister gave birth to her daughter in New York City and even though she did not have a car she needed a car seat to put into a taxi for transporting her newborn daughter back to her apartment—the hospital actually had a policy that babies cannot be released from hospital without a baby car seat. For myself, I needed to install my car seat prior to Victoria's birth to get her safely back home.

Most dads would need to install car seats in their own vehicles. A car seat for newborns generally consists of a base that is secured to one of a car's rear seats and a carrier that clips into the base. There are, of course, many other formats of child seats. There are plenty of YouTube videos on how to install the base of a baby car seat system. There are services that you can buy where someone comes to your place and installs the car seat for you. I recommend a DIY job for the install because (a) you need to know how to install and uninstall these things and (b) a service costs upward of $40 which is a rip-off for something anyone can and should learn how to do. Read and follow your car seat instructions carefully.

You will need to have a stroller to cart the baby around on foot. We used a stroller with a bassinet for Victoria's newborn phase. Strollers are great because they reduce the effort of carrying the baby while you are out for extended periods. Some car seat carriers clip into a stroller frame, which is super convenient. My wife and I do not have such a system, but we can appreciate that it is an excellent way to go as you do not need to unstrap the baby when you need to leave the car.

Slings are pretty great for carrying the baby around without a bulky stroller to contend with. Slings leave both hands free when you need to handle something. For Victoria, we mounted her on our stomachs and had her face us when we were wearing the sling.

Slings start to become useful once the baby has decent head control, which happens at around two months old. Head control is important because if you put a baby with no neck strength in a sling then the baby will slump like crazy and you will spend all of your energy and attention trying to keep her upright. Also, manufacturers of baby slings often recommend that only babies over a certain weight and height should be put into a sling, so check your product instructions carefully.

Educate yourself and your baby

It is never too early to educate your baby. One of the activities that pediatricians strongly recommend is to read to your newborn baby. It gets them used to language at a very early age. There are numerous benefits to reading to your child:

- **Reading a book to your baby turns into a special activity that you can do together.** It helps with father-child bonding. It is important for your baby to bond to you especially in the newborn-to-infant stages because this is prime time for your baby to form lifelong attachments. Your baby will be exposed to the soothing sound of your voice and it will become a calming influence for her.
- **It will help your child with language development.** Even though she does not understand the words that you are saying, the cadence, rhythm, and accent of language prepares your baby to eventually learn the skills of speaking, listening, and reading. Reading is one of the best things you can do for your baby to improve educational performance years later. Reading helps boost your baby's brain power. Your kid will have a larger vocabulary and better

math skills compared with kids who are not read to.

- **Your baby will have better emotional intelligence** if you express what you are reading with feeling.
- **If you make reading time a fun, daily event, then your baby will grow to love reading books.** A life-long love affair with reading only leads to great things for your child!

Here is the best thing: the content of what you are reading does not matter a whit, at least for the first few months. Your baby cannot understand any language so you could be reading literally anything. My trick is to read to my baby stuff that I need to learn anyway—the content does not matter. I am studying for a professional board exam these days, so I sometimes I read to her impenetrable stuff on radiation safety and irradiation calculations for medical linear accelerators. I am also reading to Victoria from a book on persuasion psychology (it's *Influence*, by Robert Cialdini, an absolute must read for any parent). So, you learn and your baby learns. Two birds, one stone. And you get to practice your deep manly reading voice as well.

Nursing system

A newborn baby's primary job is to drink a ton of milk. The parents' primary job is to feed the baby this ton of milk. Milk is required to make the baby grow from a helpless newborn to a slightly less helpless infant. Milk is what the baby is crying for more than half the time. Having an efficient feeding system is vital to your baby's well-being as well as your own sanity.

Nursing can consist of any combination of the following components: breast feeding, bottle feeding of expressed breast milk, and bottle feeding of formula. The pros and cons of each of these are:

Breast feeding

Pros: Greatest transfer of fresh antibodies from mom to baby to boost the immune system, more natural way to introduce probiotics to your baby's digestive system, enhances the bond between mother and child, babies who breast feed have been shown to display higher intelligence and advanced development compared to those who do not.

Cons: Takes a long time to breast feed (30-60 minutes), all the work is on the mother, once milk production has begun breast milk has to be removed every 3-5 hours or else there is risk for breast infection, takes a lot of work upfront as both baby and mother need to learn how to breastfeed efficiently.

Bottle feeding of expressed breast milk

Pros: Most of the antibodies in breast milk are transferred to the baby (depending on the milk's freshness), dad can act as a surrogate feeder and thus give the mom a break, much quicker to feed the baby (5-20 minutes).

Cons: Some antibodies are lost due to storage of breast milk, sterilizing bottles all the time is yet another chore, stored breast milk takes up space in your fridge, need to maintain a breast pump system.

Bottle feeding of formula:

Pros: Mom can sleep through the night because milk production has not been stimulated, can buy in bulk at the store, can be used as a bridge food while mom's milk production ramps up after birth, baby sleeps very well after formula since it digests more slowly than breast milk, unopened formula is very portable and can be used for excursions.

Cons: No natural antibodies are given to baby, costs a lot if you do it all the time, it is a hassle to maintain a bottle sterilization system (similar problem with feeding expressed breast milk from a bottle).

At our house, we used all three components for our baby during the first two months. In the right proportion the advantages of each can be enhanced without taking too much of a hit on the disadvantages. My wife breastfed Victoria during the day while I was at work—this adds up to about 6 out of 10 feedings throughout the day. When I got home from work we ate dinner together and then she went to sleep for 3-4 hours, during which time I fed Victoria once with bottled breast milk and then once with as much formula as she can handle. I tried to time the formula feed right before I hit the sack as the formula knocked her out for at least a couple of hours. During the night, my wife either breast fed our baby or fed her bottled breast milk (the latter is good if my wife just wanted to feed as fast as possible to squeeze in more sleep). We utilized all three components in a way that allowed us to have enough sleep and take care of ourselves. The baby got the vast majority of her food from breast milk and thus acquired its natural benefits, and only a small supplement of formula to bridge the gap and to help her to sleep. As Victoria got older, the proportion of breast milk increased until at two months she was exclusively breastfed.

It is universally accepted that breast milk should be the primary food source for a baby because nature put nearly every nutrient and antibody that a baby needs to grow in the stuff. This does take a lot of upfront investment in time and effort. Breastfeeding is technically a natural process that both mom and baby have some instinct on how to do it; however, there certainly is a learning process that needs to occur before baby is breastfeeding efficiently. Breastfeeding clinics are great places to learn this skill. It might take a while for the baby to stop painfully tearing at mom's nipple, learn how to get a good latch, and find out how to suck to get the milk flowing. As well, it takes a while for mom to sort out how to angle the baby to get the best latch, hold the baby so that her arms do not get tired, and find things to do during the hours of endless breastfeeding. It takes a while, but the investment is worth it.

One thing that is important to stress when coming up with a nursing system is to take into account the fact that a breastfeeding woman needs to take out her milk every 3-4 hours or else her boobs will feel like exploding. The amount of milk production will vary depending on how much the baby draws from the mother. For twins, milk production ramps up considerably to feed two babies. Since your wife needs to take out milk every 3-4 hours, you need to design your sleep rota, nursing system, and all the other things in your life around that schedule.

It is worthwhile to have a discussion with your wife prior to the baby's birth about how you will feed your baby. We didn't, and we scrambled the first week trying to figure out how to feed Victoria. The pros and cons listed above for breastfeeding, bottle nursing with expressed breast milk, and bottle nursing with formula will help you weigh your decisions.

You will likely need a baby bottle system, so let's talk about how to set one up. Baby bottle systems are so important because it allows the father to be a surrogate feeder for the mother. With breast pump technology, you can mechanically express breast milk into containers for feeding at a later time. Formula can also be used to supplement breast milk. If you have a great baby bottle system, then this will make your life much, much easier. If you do not have a good baby bottle system, this will probably be the most frustrating thing you will deal with as a new parent. The following overviews what I think is a well-optimized baby bottle system.

First, you need to go shopping. You will need a breast pump, nursery bottles, and a drying rack. We used a breast pump with disposable, pre-sterilized bags. These pumps come in single (one boob) or double (two boobs at the same time) pump configurations. They are quite expensive, but they pay themselves many times over. The disposable bag system is awesome because you do not have to worry about sterilizing breast milk storage containers again and again. These bags have handy volume markings in ounces and mL on the side. You will need to get at least four breast cups and pump connectors (the things that connect the boobs to the breast pump) to use in your rotation.

For bottles, we used the PlayTex disposable liner nurser (baby bottle) system. A single nurser consists of an outer shell where a disposable, pre-sterilized milk liner drops in. A nipple screws in over the top and seals the liner. The disposable liners are awesome for the same reason as the milk bags—less things to sterilize. You will need about six bottle shells/nipples, and about a hundred liners per month. It is important to only use one type of nurser bottle. If you have several different brands of nursers you will get frustrated with mismatched items that do not fit with each other.

You will need a baby-safe detergent to wash milk or formula off of the bottles and breast pump components. It is useful to have a bottle scrubber set as well.

You will need a drying rack for the bottles and breast pump components. We use the Boon Lawn drying rack—it looks like a bunch of plastic spikes close together that you stick all your sterilized stuff on. This rack is probably the most useful baby product I have purchased.

You will need a sterilizer. We boil water in a stock pot dedicated to our baby bottle system and put all the bottle and breast pump components in for five minutes. It does the trick. You can also buy commercial sterilizers, but I heard those are kind of expensive so we did not bother. You will also need a pair of tongs to pull stuff out of boiling water.

Last of all, you need a ***system*** to have this all running smoothly. You can have the entire kit as described above and still have things fall apart on you. You need to figure out the following problems to make your nursing system run smoothly:

- Where do the dirty nurser and breast pump components go?
- Where do the washed (but not sterilized) components go?
- Where do the sterilized (but not dry) components go?
- Where do the sterilized and dry components go?
- How do you warm up refrigerated breast milk and/or formula?

Here is our step-by-step system at my house:

1. As nurser and breast pump components get used and dirty, we place them by the sink until enough parts accumulate to warrant a sterilizing cycle.
2. I use detergent and bottle sponges to clean all of the components in the sink and then place them in a large bowl. While I am doing this, I start a pot of boiling water on the stove. By the time I have washed everything, the water is close to a boil.
3. I then dump all of the parts that need to be sterilized into the boiling water. (Note: we use the Playtex nurser system—the outer hard plastic shell that holds the disposable liner just needs to be cleaned and not sterilized, so we don't bother boiling this shell). Everything needs to be boiled for 5 minutes to kill off any germs. I stick the ends of the tongs in for a couple of minutes to make sure that these are clean.
4. I set the Boon Lawn drying rack nearby the stove and pull out all of the sterilized parts with the tongs. I then dump the boiling water as having it around is a hazard.
5. I move the drying rack to a low-traffic spot in our kitchen. It takes a couple of hours to dry.
6. Once dry, I assemble the breast pump components and put them in a clean plastic bag in the nursery beside the breast pump, so my wife can easily access her entire pump system (which is always at hand, plugged in, and ready for

action beside her nursing chair). I assemble the Playtex nurser system, placing the nipples in the retainer rings, putting the disposable liner in the nurser shell, and screwing everything together.

7. For warming up refrigerated breast milk or formula, we have an electric kettle with some water in it on standby. I hit the ON button on the kettle and then after it gets hot I pour it into a bowl with a little cold water. I test the temperature to see if it is warm, and then set a bottle full of breast milk/formula in it to warm up.

The above system sounds pretty straightforward and common sense, and I apologize if you already figured this out. I mention all of these steps in detail because as new parents this took us a couple of weeks to figure out in its entirety. We thought that since we had all the pieces in our house we were alright, but the thing that we were missing was ***the system***. Before we figured this out I nearly had a meltdown trying to settle my crying baby while trying to find enough sterilized parts to assemble a bottle! I want to stress the importance of having a great system to make breast pumping and bottle feeding as easy as possible.

Things will also change as your baby develops. By our daughter's third month, she was exclusively breastfeeding. We let this happen naturally. Fortunately, the increase in breastfeeding corresponded to Victoria sleeping more and more throughout the night, so my wife was able to handle the increased breastfeeding load. At that point, we retired our baby bottle system.

By six months, your baby should have started with solid food. Keep communicating with your baby's physician to determine the best diet for your baby's stage of development.

This may look like a common kitchen, but it is actually a well-tuned battle station for cleaning baby bottles and breast pump components. (a) Designated place for used bottles and breast pump equipment; (b) Baby safe detergent; (c) Bottle sponges; (d) Stainless steel bowl for putting washed items; (e) Sterilization equipment; (f) Drying rack; (g) Designated place to put assembled bottles.

Burping and farting

As a husband and new father, you are the Burper-In-Chief and Farter-In-Chief. Fortunately, burping and farting your baby is easy.

Burps and farts are just gas pockets trapped within the baby's gastrointestinal system. If the path of least resistance is upwards, gas is released as a burp; if the best way out is downwards, you get a fart. Babies need to burp and fart because babies are uncomfortable having gas bloating up their insides (just like us big people). Victoria had gas problems most acutely between 2-6 weeks old. She would cry like crazy until we got the gas out.

The way to de-gas your baby is to essentially perturb the gas until it finds its way out of either end of your baby. Burping is relatively easy. Simply holding your newborn upright against you with her head resting on your shoulder is usually sufficient. Gas travels upwards due to buoyancy so just holding her in this upright position works really well. Sometimes light patting or rubbing on the back helps the gas to come out. Pat or rub lightly, no need to whack the baby. Usually a baby needs to be burped after a feed. Bottles are particularly bad for gas retention because the baby always swallows some air as she is finishing off the bottle.

Farting your baby is not too hard either. My main method to do this is to lie my baby on her back and slowly pump her legs towards and away from her stomach. Victoria thinks this is fun exercise. The pumping action compresses her little belly so that the gas works its way downwards until it forms a fart. Newborn farts fortunately do not smell bad because babies this young have not yet developed the gut flora that causes bowels to become a nasty swamp of decay such as found in adults.

Newborn babies burp like drunk sailors on leave looking for a good time at port. Newborn babies fart like middle-aged men at their worst behavior. The noises that newborns make are equivalent to what you would expect to come out of gross, unwashed adults with no manners, shame, or dignity.

In a way, it is hilarious to hear my adorable Victoria burp and fart like a champ. You may be amazed at how your darling daughter or cute little son can make such rude noises. Just know that it is healthy and good for them to expel this gas from their bodies. And hope that your baby does not burp or fart in too many public places since most people will assume that you are the one with the coarse manners.

Sleep

In the beginning, your baby will be waking up all the time. Night and day was a blurry concept in the womb, so this non-conformance to diurnal rhythms continues after birth. During this early stage, parents need to just work around her sleep patterns with an appropriate sleep rota (refer back to the earlier chapter on this topic back in the Self-Care part of the book). This pattern of short sleep durations will continue until a baby starts to learn how to sleep through the night.

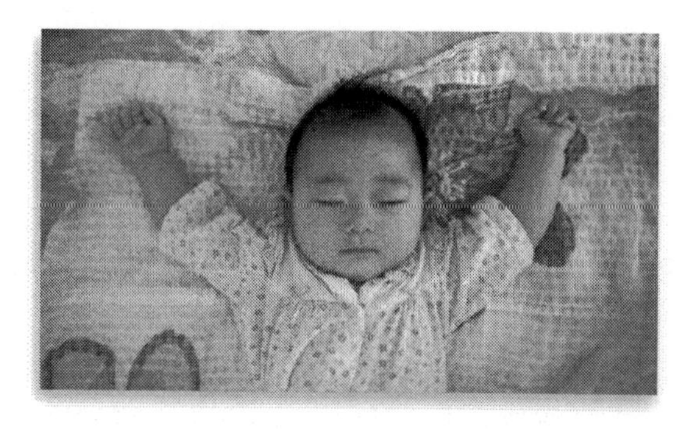

Sleep is awesome!

You will often be asked if your baby has started to sleep through the night. "Sleeping through the night" has different definitions, but let's just say this means sleeping six hours straight at night. It is in everyone's best benefit to get to that point as soon as possible. My Victoria started sleeping through the night at about 10 weeks of age, but I read that this can take up to six months for this to occur.

I am not really sure how Victoria figured out how to sleep through the night so early, she just started to do it. I have a few suspicions on how this happened:

- Around 9 P.M., my wife and I go through a bedtime ritual that is the same every night.
- The ritual includes: family time in bed together playing with Victoria, reading a short book with lots of pictures, our baby getting a breast feeding, changing her diaper, me rocking and singing our baby to sleep, and then settling her down gently.
- Whether my wife is breastfeeding or I am bottle feeding we really try to fill our baby up as much as possible for her evening feed.
- When I sing to my baby (off-tune, of course), I always sing the same songs. Greatest hits include "Baa, Baa, Black Sheep", "Twinkle, Twinkle, Little Star", and "Alphabet Song" (these are good because they all have the same melody). I also sing some ridiculous baby songs I made up such as "Yoga Baby" and "Korean Side Dishes" (this one is in Korean).
- As full-grown adults, we love to sleep through the night, so there is little ambient stimulation unless the baby wakes herself up.

- We tend to play with our baby a lot in the evenings so perhaps that tires our little one so that she is more amenable to sleeping for longer.
- Victoria seems to sleep better when she has had her evening bath.

This seems to be in line with everything that I have read about training your baby to sleep through the night. From my own experience and from reading lots of resource materials, I think that the two main keys to training your baby to sleep at night are:

1. Play with her lots a couple of hours before bedtime.
2. Have relaxing rituals like bathing, feeding, singing, and rocking right before bed.

Baby sleep patterns will eventually become synergistic to your own. When the baby sleeps, it is much easier for parents to also get some sleep, and vice versa. It is a natural process, just try to help it along as much as you can.

Bathing your baby

Newborn babies do not need to be bathed very often. Once every two to three days is sufficient. Newborns spend their time in nice clean cribs, play mats, and parents' arms. Solid food does not enter into the picture for newborns so there is no issue with food getting slathered all over them. There is no rolling around in the grass outside. Newborn babies are pretty clean creatures for the most part. Even their poo is not that smelly. This is good news to busy new dads and moms because they do not need to be bathed every day. It is actually a good idea to not bathe your newborn baby every day because that can actually dry out their sensitive skin.

Sponge bath procedure

For the first one or two weeks, give your baby a sponge bath. These are quite easy to do. For setup, have two baby bath towels on standby at arm's length, at least three baby rags, and some baby soap. You can either do a sponge bath over a sink, over a basin full of warm water, or a combination of both. I did sponge baths over the sink with running warm water. The water temperature should be appropriate. To find this out, dip your forearm or elbow in the water and if your skin feels like it is the same temperature as the water then you are good.

Have a couple of clean baby rags on hand. Use the rags to wash the face first, starting around the eyes, then moving to the forehead, cheeks, and mouth. Avoid getting water inside the ears as this is a major risk for infection. Clean the rest of the body, being sure to get inside the skin folds. Pay special attention to the neck and armpits as lots of breast milk spillage collects there. Avoid getting the umbilical cord stump wet. Wash hands and feet thoroughly as well. Immediately after finishing, wrap your baby in the two bath towels to keep her core temperature stable. Dress her when dry.

When the umbilical cord stump falls off, then you can switch to a tub bath. You can do this in a sink basin, but I prefer doing it in a plastic infant tub because by the time it came to tub bathing Victoria could wave her arms and legs quite vigorously and both our kitchen and bathroom sinks have hard irregular metal parts that our baby can bang herself on.

Tub baths are best done with two people involved. This is how we do it.

Tub bath procedure

I fill the infant tub half full with warm water, using the forearm test to determine if the water temperature is appropriate. My wife grabs the following: baby foam soap, baby-safe moisturizer, zinc oxide barrier cream, at least three baby rags, two towels, and our changing pad. The two towels are draped on the changing pad at the ready for drying our baby. We do everything on the floor because it is safer.

My wife and I strip Victoria down to her diaper. I hold my baby over the tub while my wife uses a baby rag to wash her hair with baby soap. She then gets another rag and cleans the baby's face (with no soap this time). We then move her to the changing pad, dry her hair with the towels, and strip off her diaper.

My next job is to pick up Victoria and immerse her in the tub water, being very careful support her head and neck to keep the head and especially her ears out of the water (remember the ear infection hazard). My wife uses one baby rag soaked in warm water to cover our baby's belly to keep it warm since her belly is out of the water. She uses another rag to clean everywhere with a bit of baby soap, ensuring that she gets all the creases and folds.

Then I lift her out of the water, set her down on top of the towels, and immediately wrap our baby in both towels to keep her temperature up. We make sure her head is also covered with the towels. We have these baby towels with hoodies attached to them, I find these really handy to cover Victoria's head after a bath.

After that we slap on some zinc oxide cream in her diaper area, apply a light coating of moisturizer on her body (avoiding the hands, face, and feet) and clothe her.

Our baby freaking loves bath time. It calms her down and gets her drowsy afterwards. It is a nice family bonding activity. My wife and I work as a team during bath time so it is a bonding experience for us as well.

Some safety tips on bathing your baby:

- Always, always hold your baby while in the bath.

- Never leave a baby in the bathtub alone.
- Never leave standing water in a tub unattended.
- Never leave your baby in a bathtub that is filling up with water, for obvious reasons that the water might get too deep, too hot, or too cold. Fill the bathtub first, test water temperature, then bathe, in that order.
- Put your common sense safety hat on—it's water, after all, and water can be dangerous.

Bath time can be the highlight of your family's day as you are all doing something together as a team. It also gets the baby sleepy and ready for bed, so it is a good ritual before bedtime.

Baby play

Baby play involves a baby looking at and eventually handling and sucking toys. It sounds pretty basic, but baby play is an extremely important developmental activity. Play teaches a baby visual and aural acuity, color recognition, hand dexterity, hand-eye coordination, and mental focus.

It is a good idea to get a few low-cost items to facilitate baby play. Focus charts are useful for the baby's first few weeks while she cannot really do anything but look around. Right when the baby is born, she can barely see. Sharp contrast black and white focus charts placed near her can help your baby focus. When you notice your baby start to take an interest in colorful objects, you can switch to color focus charts. You do not really need to buy these things, you can just download focus charts online and print them out. Focus charts keep a very young newborn entertained and provide valuable targets for visual stimulation.

It is well worth it to invest in a baby gym. Baby gyms are arches that hang toys over a baby lying on her back. Usually a mat is incorporated into the gym for the baby to lie down on. Some of the fancier electronic baby gyms have flashing lights and music that plays when the baby strikes a button, key, or surface. The toys that dangle over the baby are always colorful to aid in the development of visual acuity and depth perception. Toys have dangling ends for the baby to practice grabbing.

Some baby gyms have a dangling mirror for babies to see themselves—babies totally love mirrors.

Baby gyms are very useful for the busy parent, as you can set the baby down in the gym and she will amuse herself while getting valuable tactile, visual, and aural stimulation. I have read that newborns can start with the baby gym at any time; however, I really did not find them practical until around the six week mark.

Victoria playing in her baby gym.

Books for newborn babies are excellent for facilitating baby play. Lots of these books are made of soft cloth with colorful prints on them. My Victoria loves looking at the colorful pictures in these books. I like reading to her from these books, often going off script and pointing out various objects in the pictures. I am hoping that by starting her early with these baby books she will develop a love for reading.

Finally, there is Peek-a-Boo. My wife tells me that Peek-a-Boo is somehow critical for a baby's development. I say, whatever, it is just a hilarious game to play for both dad and baby.

Equipment: One baby rag. Method: Cover face with rag. Remove rag quickly and say, "Peek-a-Boo!" I swear, you can do Peek-a-Boo a million times and a baby will still think it is awesome.

Calming

You need to find ways to calm your baby. Your sanity depends on it. Crying takes its toll on both baby and parents. If parents do not know how to calm their baby, then this persistent crying will cause exhaustion, depression, and marital disharmony. In such a state, parents can act badly and even put the baby in danger—how can an exasperated and exhausted parent effectively hold a baby without tripping over furniture or dropping her? Also, babies need to be calm to develop well—how can a baby breastfeed, learn language cadences, or practice motor skills when she is bawling her head off all the time? Calming is an absolutely essential skill for new moms and dads.

So, without further ado, here are my Nuclear Weapons for calming my baby girl. Try these on your little one, some of them are bound to work!

Anthony's Nuclear Weapons for Calming Baby Victoria

Swaddling

Swaddling worked great for the first three weeks. Swaddling is supposed to simulate the snug environment of the womb to calm the baby. Swaddling also made it easier to handle the baby as everything is bundled up nice and tight. After about the one month mark, Victoria started to straighten her legs and move them around. At that point it was tough to keep her in a swaddle but by then Victoria did not really need it to keep calm.

Side-to-Side Motion

Swinging from side-to-side is great for calming a baby down. Just hold her in your arms and swing her to and fro in a gentle manner. We have a couple of baby swings (of the four that we borrowed from friends) that worked reasonably well to keep our baby calm; however, if she is crying and fussy, only human contact calms her down. Baby swings are useful if you need to put your already-calm newborn down for a few minutes while you need to do something else.

Exercise stability ball

These bouncy balls work wonders to calm Victoria and also many other newborns. With your baby in your arms, sit comfortably on the stability ball with legs wide apart. Gently and slowly bounce up and down. Your baby will love the jiggly motion. My daughter calms down immediately when I use this technique. If the stability ball is not around, no problem: I simply do mini-squats to simulate the bouncy motion, kind of like a slow-motion Gangnam Style horse-trot. This is great exercise for your core muscles, so you get a bonus. Make sure that you do not move too fast as you do not want to cause any brain damage.

Breastfeeding

Breastfeeding is hands down the best way to calm the baby with sucking. Babies love to suck on things. Another thing that worked is that sometimes I would just let Victoria suck on her hands to occupy herself. When she got a little more coordinated she started sucking on her toes.

Singing

Singing is an excellent way to calm down a baby. Singing also helps calm a baby down. I have read that if you sing to the baby while still in the womb, the baby will remember the songs you sing and will find solace from them even after birth. I am a terrible singer and I mangle all the words to both English and Korean nursery rhymes, but I can still calm down my baby. If you cannot sing, shushing also works—just emulate a noisy vacuum cleaner.

Special-holding-technique-thingy

Probably the most effective calming position for Victoria is with me holding Victoria lying on her stomach draped over my forearm, with my hand cupping her face to support her head. It is like magic: she always instantly calmed down. I do not need to move her around in this position, I just need to hold her steady. I call this the "special-holding-technique-thingy". After about five seconds, I bring baby back into a standard football cradling position, calm as a cucumber.

Going outside

Simply taking my daughter outside instantly transforms a crying baby into a tranquil one. It works magic on my Victoria. I am not certain why this works, but I would hazard a guess that a baby gets tired of being cooped up inside and enjoys the fresh air, rustling of the leaves, and bright colors of the outdoors. Hey, it works so I'll take it.

Putting her in comfort zones

Victoria has her comfort zones around the house. She loves to be on her changing table because it is where she gets cleaned up and she can see the nice colorful pictures on the walls of the nursery. In her first month, she loved to be in her play pen. Later on, she enjoyed lying in our bed with us beside her as it was our family time together. Figure out where your baby's comfort zones are around your home and rely upon them to calm your baby.

Focus charts and colorful books

As mentioned in the previous chapter on play, visual stimulation is great for exercising a baby's visual cortex and has the added bonus of calming her down. Before a baby is a month old, she will like seeing high contrast images like checkerboard patterns or simple black-and-white pictures. These images would fascinate our baby so we would set these up in her crib or playpen for her to look at them. After a month, a baby can begin to discern colors. Victoria was very interested in colorful children's books so we would read them to her when she started to get cranky. Our most effective go-to book was the page-turning thriller, "If I Were a Rabbit", which I must have read to her fifty times.

Baby mobile

We have an electronic baby mobile that lights up with various colors, rotates, and plays music. We have it attached to her crib. When we turn it on, it is like crack cocaine for her. She does this cute thing where she puts her hands behind her head and looks at the spinning mobile in childlike wonderment. See if you can find some similar automated visual stimulation (something that is not a tablet or a smart phone, of course).

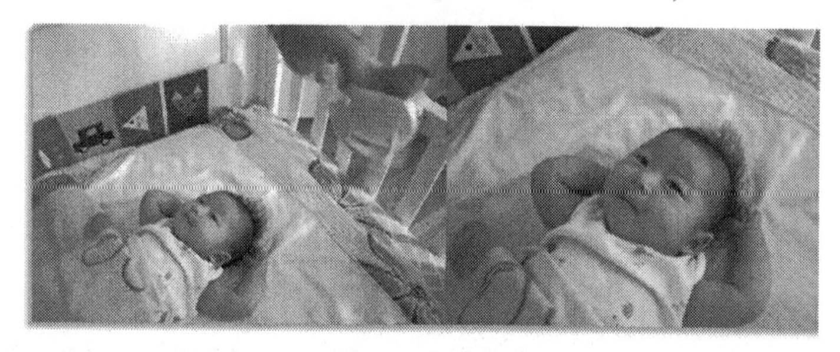

Left: Victoria watching her mobile having a good time. Right: Victoria looking at her dad in irritation because he is taking too many cell phone pictures.

Different things work for different babies. The exercise stability ball trick works wonders for my daughter, but does not for another baby that my wife knows. Our baby's favorite spots in our house are specific to her. Over the first month, you will find out what the best tricks are to calm your baby.

One pretty universal trick is to drive your newborn around the block endless times. This is a tried and true method to stop a baby's crying, though it is a pain in the ass and a huge time suck. I never do this because I do not have the time and I don't like wasting money on gas. Try to develop time-efficient and easy-to-use methods for calming.

I have read about the cry-it-out method to train babies to self-soothe. The basic principle is to allow the baby to bawl her head off for a pre-determined time prior to swooping in to comfort the baby. Now I am no pediatrician and I am sure that there is some scientific backing for this method, but this just sounds too painful to me as a parent and I would not want to put my baby through that. In fact, all of our health care professionals told us that "cry-it-out" is not the way to go. I prefer to do things the easier and more stress-free way. My wife and I calm our baby down as soon as she starts showing distress. I feel that this builds trust between us and the baby. And our baby is generally quite easy to handle, which I attribute to attentive parenting when our baby needs us.

Calming is one of the most important skills for a new dad to have. President Barack Obama has been caught on camera lots of times calming babies at the events that he attends—check out some of these videos on YouTube. He is really, really good at it. This guy was the leader of the free world but he is also a father to two girls. Even he had to master the art of calming a baby. Becoming an expert at baby calming will make for a much happier family life.

Growth spurts

The first growth spurt took us totally by surprise because we did not know about them. Victoria all of a sudden had to feed every hour and was a very fussy lady if she did not get her way. She would barely sleep. We thought there was something wrong, until we learned about growth spurts.

Much of a baby's growth happens in intense bursts that occur approximately at three weeks, six weeks, nine weeks, three months, six months, and nine months. Babies do not read calendars so these spurts can really happen at any time. A growth spurt usually lasts between 24-48 hours. Babies are cranky, sleep a lot less, and want to eat all the time.

Growth spurts are annoying because you think you finally figured out the baby's schedule and then you get whacked over the head with this irregular behaviour. You cannot beat biology, but you can get through your first growth spurt using these tricks:

- Recognize when a growth spurt is happening so that you can prepare effectively for it. Babies tend to sleep A LOT right before a growth spurt. Also, you know the approximate times when these tend to happen so you know to look out for it.

- Stock the fridge with prepared food so that most of your time and your wife's time is allocated to baby care.
- Give your wife lots of water to drink—if you drink bottled water have a stock of bottles at your nursing stations.
- Make sure that nursing and diaper systems are optimized.
- Make sure that you have mastered a few calming techniques.

Growth spurts are a tough but you need to power through them. With the above preparation, these periods will go by a little bit more smoothly. Just recognize what they are and realize that they will pass in a couple of days.

Get professional photography

Your baby is super cute. Like, the cutest thing you have ever seen. The cutest baby in the whole world.

In the whirlwind that is the first three months of a baby's life, it is easy to forget that she will never be this tiny and adorable again. Babies grow FAST. Before you know it she will be a gangly teenager with acne and trying to break out of the house all the time. Capture her newborn cuteness by arranging for professional photography.

Cell phone photography is great to capture all of the spontaneous moments; however, you truly need professional baby photography to put something up on a wall for posterity.

No matter how hard I try, I cannot produce a photo as good as these:

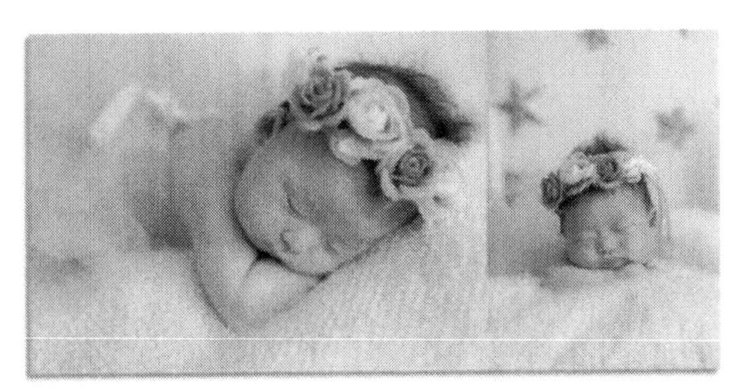

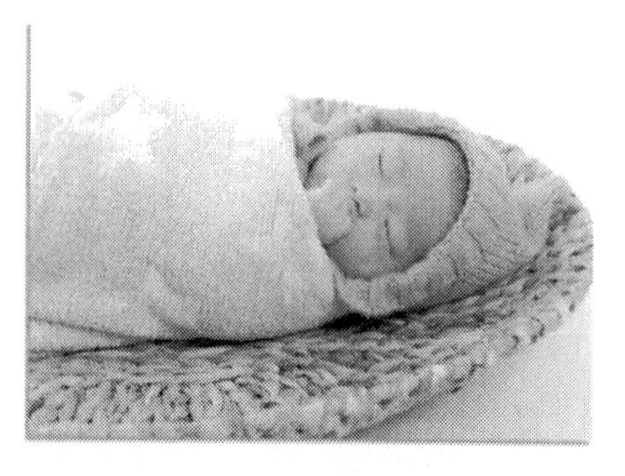

See what I mean? ISN'T SHE TOTALLY PRECIOUS? CUTEST BABY IN THE WORLD!!!

OK, getting carried away now. I have been accused of being a *dal babo*, which in the Korean language is roughly translated as "dad who totally loves his daughter." Reining it in now.

I hope you see what I mean. I take blurry cell phone pictures. You can totally hang the above professionally-produced images on a wall.

I totally recommend that you get professional photography. It is worth every penny.

We got ours done with Victoria's chubby cheeks already come in; however, I have seen some great shots of newborns in their first couple of weeks and they are equally adorable. Capture a moment that will never come again in your kid's life.

Have fun with your baby and be happy!

I strongly believe that if my wife and I are happy, well-adjusted, and loving around our newborn daughter then she will grow up to be a happy, well-adjusted, and loving person.

We think of child-rearing as an incredible gift. All of the hard work to take care of a baby does not really feel like work at all. I look forward to every smile my baby gives me. I look forward to changing her soiled diaper because I know that means she is healthy and growing. I look forward to coaxing new developments from my daughter. I even look forward to calming her down when she is fussy because I know that will strengthen the bonds of love and trust between us.

I have a lot of fun with Victoria. I think she is hilarious. As I write this penultimate chapter, Victoria is almost four months old. When I say, "Where's my little girl's smile?" she hits me with a huge grin. Making her laugh is a lot of fun. I recently found out that flying her around the house Superman-style makes her burst out in laughter. It is so funny hearing chuckles come from such a small human being.

I love helping her improve her hand dexterity by giving her different things to grip. She is learning the sound of her voice and sometimes copies the sounds that my wife and I make. We call her "yoga baby" because she can now grab her feet with her hands and put her feet over her head. For some reason she loves this position and can hold it for several minutes. Victoria is now excelling at tummy time and can hold her head up no problem. She can even do Upward Dog.

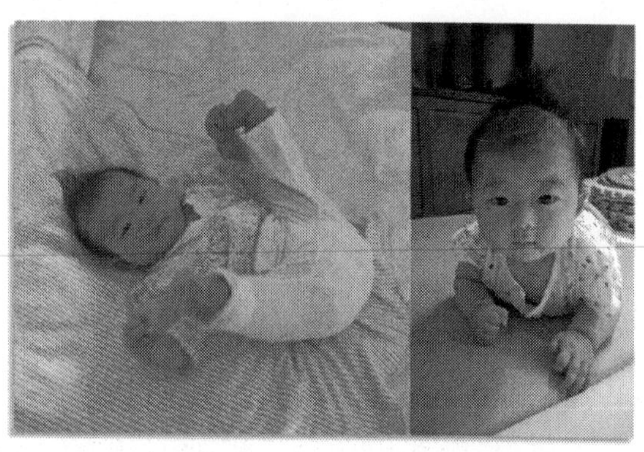

Left: Yoga Baby; Right: Upward Dog! (well... close enough)

Having fun with your baby makes all the hard work not really work at all. All of the life hacks in this book are meant to help a man make the sharp transition into fatherhood much more smoothly.

Even if all these tips and tricks are effective in streamlining your life, it will all still seem like a chore unless you employ one last hack:

Have fun with your baby and be happy!

Baby-care recap

In this final part of this book, we took a look at the basic mechanics of taking care of a baby. There are so many other materials out there online or in the bookstore, but these are the basics to make your life easier.

- Systems are everything. Optimize as many systems as you can as fast as you can before and after the baby arrives.
- Diaper changes are a cinch once you optimize your diaper changing battle station.
- Poo. It is gross. Just learn to deal with it.
- No matter what you do, don't drop the baby. Use the primitive part of your man brain to ensure that you never, ever drop the baby. Instill a safety culture in your home.
- Car seats, strollers, and slings are necessary to cart your little one around town. Learn how to assemble and deploy these—they will be your new best friends.
- Educate yourself and your baby. Read to your baby and play with her as much as possible.
- Your nursing system needs to be optimized, especially if you are using baby bottles.
- Burping and farting is easy.
- Sleep is important for your whole family. Hopefully your baby gets attuned to nocturnal rhythms quickly.

- Bathing your baby is relatively simple and a fun time for the whole family.
- Baby play is really important for development.
- Calming techniques are incredibly important for everyone's overall sanity.
- Growth spurts are annoying. Just recognize them for what they are when you see them and power through them.
- Get professional photography. Totally worth it!
- Last tip: Have fun with your baby and be happy!

To be continued...

Becoming a father is one of the most transformative and amazing experiences a man can have. I believe that there is a choice every father needs to make: either take action to make this time awesome, fulfilling, and peaceful, or leave everything to chance. In reading this book, you are making a choice to thrive during the transition to fatherhood.

There are lots of resources that are out there to guide new moms through pregnancy, childbirth, and motherhood; however, there is not much out there to guide new fathers. I hope this guide helped you gain knowledge for the road ahead.

Remember: it is vital to take care of all three members of your family. **Self-care** is critical to become the rock of the family after your wife has gone through the hell of childbirth. **Wife-care** is so important to keep up your partner's vitality during one of the most difficult physical and mental challenges of her life. **Baby-care** done right is key to getting your child off to the best start possible.

The contents of this book are all the life hacks I employed to make my own transition to fatherhood an awesome experience. My goal was to focus on those elements of new fatherhood that I thought could be optimized to make life many times easier compared to un-optimized systems. As men, we like to solve problems. I actually had fun figuring out all the different tips and tricks to make my family's life much easier.

Who knows, if enough men find this book useful and there is demand for it perhaps I will write "A Man's Guide to Infants". If that does well, perhaps next up will be "A Man's Guide to Toddlers", then eventually "A Man's Guide to Gangly, Acne-Ridden, and Rebellious Teenagers".

I would love to hear feedback on my book. I have a blog discussing many topics of fatherhood at ADadsGuide.org. Please participate in the comments and forum of this website and join in a growing community of new fathers trying to be the best they can be.

I hope all the best for you and your new family. Godspeed and good luck!

-Anthony Kim

Also by Anthony Kim
Buy Now on Amazon Kindle or Paperback!

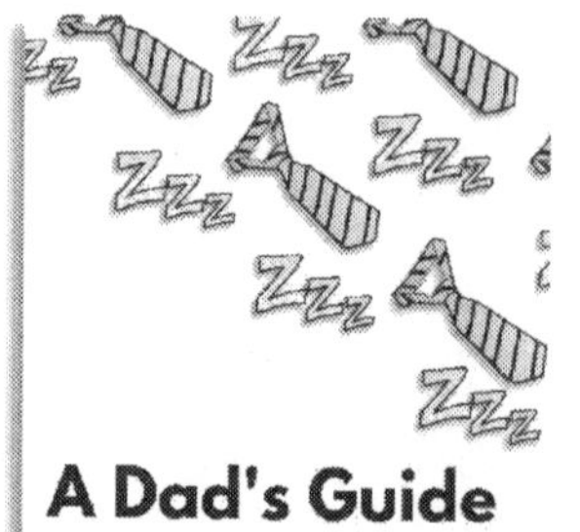

The essential guide to Great Sleep for dads of all ages!

Great Sleep is possible no matter the stage that your kids are at. Learn the mindset, Sleep Habits, and scheduling tips to get Great Sleep!

COMING SOON!

Discover the secrets to carving out huge amounts of spare time so that you can work on your projects and spend time with your family!

Subscribe to my blog and get a chance to **win this book for free**!

A final kind request...

Word-of-mouth is crucial for any author to succeed.

If you enjoyed the book, **I would greatly appreciate it if you would give a favorable rating ★★★★★ and review on Amazon--** even a sentence or two makes all the difference.

Many thanks in advance!

-Anthony Kim

A Man's Guide to Newborn Babies

By Anthony Kim

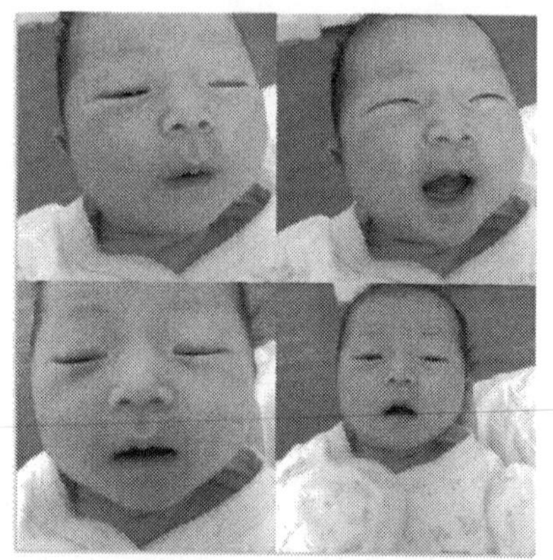

Begun: Victoria, age four weeks.

Completed: Victoria, age four months.